ENDORSEMENTS

Sharee Dorsett is a warrior! *Small but Mighty* is going to give you a vision for taking your kids beyond the shallow end of the deep pool and illustrate the importance of investing in your children so they can be all that God created them to be!

JAMIE GALLOWAY
Author of *Secrets of the Seer* and *Hearing God's Voice*
jamiegalloway.com

Sharee Dorsett's Small but Mighty is a powerful tool in the hands of parents, caregivers, teachers, and anyone who cares for children. Not only does this book breakdown a very serious and heavy topic in understandable knowledge for our kids, it also empowers them to take their destiny and purpose into their own hands. It equips them to fight demonic forces at a level they can understand. The activations and prayers at the end of the chapters guide parents to train up their children in the way they should go. *Small but Mighty* is a definite must-read!

APOSTLE DESIREE FOX
New Heart Ministries, Newark, Delaware
Regional Leader, CIAN Mid-Atlantic
Region for Christian International

It is no secret that the enemy is waging war against our children, for he understands far too well that they are our future and the arrows by which we advance the Kingdom of Light. In a world of challenges, a clear and pure voice is needed to speak a resounding word as it relates to our children—this book is that voice. With simplicity yet weighty words, Sharee Dorsett takes you into the depths of recognizing who your children are in the army of God and empowers them to wear their armor daily to wage effective warfare.

ADRIANNA P. SIMON
Intercessor, Staff Pastor, Author

Each generation of parents finds themselves facing cultural pressures pushing against their child. Some are subtle, some are obvious but all push against children to mold them into young adults without the self-assurance of who they are and what their purpose in life is. In *Small but Mighty*, Sharee places a powerful tool in the hands of parents. This book gives a well-thought-out and scripturally balanced approach to building a strong relationship with your children, helping them see and strengthen their identity and purpose. *Small but Mighty* also provides the insights your children need to stand against the elements that push against them with lies and deception. I am grateful to Sharee Dorsett for sharing her heart and wisdom she has gained on her life journey with Christ. I highly recommend this book.

ROBERT MUNCY, Apostolic Leader
The House of Praise for all People, Greenwood, Delaware
Convening Apostle, Global Alliance
for Kingdom Advancement

I've never in my life seen a book like this! It has come at such a crucial time in our society. Sharee shares her own incredible journey on how to really train up your child—not just to have good manners and be a good person, but to also know how to overcome the enemy! This book is a must-read for teachers, parents, grandparents, aunts and uncles. If you have any young people in your life, grab this book! Our kids need to be equipped to fight and WIN the battle. As a homeschool mom of a 10-year-old, I absolutely loved this one—and I know you will too.

JENNY WEAVER
Worship Leader, Author
Jenny Weaver Worships

I have had the privilege of knowing Sharee and Arnold Dorsett for more than ten years now. They have been consistently Christ-centered in their marriage, family, and ministry. The spirit of excellence is on them and all through *Small but Mighty*. What's makes this book so powerful is the truth in it and the timing of it. This is a now word for the church that Jesus is building. Because they are parents and pastors, they are practitioners. This isn't just theology, it's an autobiography. There is a spiritual authority on this book because they live what Sharee wrote. We will be using this book to help equip the parents of Rescue Church.

ADAM LiVECCHi, Senior Pastor
Rescue Church Founder, We See Jesus Ministries
Author of *Go, Preach, Heal*

I am so excited to see this new and fresh approach to spiritual warfare being published. It is out of the fires of adversity and tests that this book has been forged in the heart and mind of Sharee. I believe it will become an essential tool for parents and grandparents in preparing and raising a new generation of overcomers so they may be bright lights in a very dark culture.

KATHI OATES
Healing Brokenhearted Ministr

SMALL BUT MIGHTY

A GUIDE TO EQUIPPING YOUR CHILDREN FOR

SPIRITUAL WARFARE

SHAREE DORSETT

DESTINY IMAGE® PUBLISHERS, INC.

P.O. Box 310, Shippensburg, PA 17257-0310

"Promoting Inspired Lives."

This book and all other Destiny Image and Destiny Image Fiction books are available at Christian bookstores and distributors worldwide.

Cover design by Eileen Rockwell
Interior design by Terry Clifton

For more information on foreign distributors, call 717-532-3040.

Reach us on the Internet: www.destinyimage.com.

ISBN 13 TP: 978-0-7684-5198-6
ISBN 13 eBook: 978-0-7684-5199-3
ISBN 13 HC: 978-0-7684-5222-8
ISBN 13 LP: 978-0-7684-5221-1

For Worldwide Distribution, Printed in the U.S.A.

1 2 3 4 5 6 7 8 / 24 23 22 21 20

DEDICATIONS

I dedicate this book first to my four beautiful children who give me a reason to be a better person every day. Kamryn, Kristian, Mycah, and Moriah it's because of you that this book exists and now many families throughout the world can have a resource guide to make complicated spiritual concepts simpler.

To my amazing husband who has been my biggest fan. You believed and saw greatness in me way before I believed it myself. You have been the tool Heaven has used to sharpen and unconditionally love me. Knowing I have you by my side makes building Kingdom strongholds so much more meaningful.

To my father, thanks for giving me pit bull tenacity; my mother for showing me what unconditional love looks like; my two sisters for being the best confidants a person could ask for; and my two brothers for their consistent encouragement; and even though we are blood, still honoring the prophet over being big sis.

To my City of Love family, aka "City Shakers," I am a better person because I was given the honor to lead such an amazing group of radical city shakers. We are just beginning and the best is yet to come—love you all.

CONTENTS

Foreword. 1

Introduction 3

CHAPTER ONE   Rules of Warfare. 11

CHAPTER TWO   The Kingdom of Darkness Made Simple . . . 43

CHAPTER THREE   Curiosity Can Open Doors. 67

CHAPTER FOUR   The Enemy Is at the Gate 83

CHAPTER FIVE   Identity Is a Weapon 103

CHAPTER SIX   Hearing God as a Child 125

CHAPTER SEVEN   The Word Is a Weapon 137

CHAPTER EIGHT   Breaking Generational Cycles, Early. 151

CHAPTER NINE   Punishment Versus Discipline. 163

CHAPTER TEN   Love, The Most Powerful Tool on Earth . . 191

Conversation Starter Tips 205

Resource Tool Box 207

A Few Words Explained. 209

Topical Scripture Guide 213

Sources Cited. 215

FOREWORD

There is an unseen battle raging over the destiny of every human being ever born. Each and every person carries a unique purpose and calling, and each has a distinct personality and expression. If you put two people in the same lane, they will both execute it differently. This is part of the beauty and mystery of Christ and His amazing Body.

We understand these concepts within the context of adulthood, but what about infants and children? What about the personalities that begin to emerge at the youngest age? What about the challenges and demonic attacks that occur in the lives of children? Why does the devil strike when they are most vulnerable? He is trying to abort the fulfillment of their calling by painting a false concept of who they are, who God is, and what the plan is for their life. He does not wait until they reach adulthood to attack their assignment. He begins immediately.

I have sat with countless parents praying over their children at all stages of life and development. I have seen the tears that pour through a parent who is dealing with heavy attacks against their child. We need tools that address this warfare and equip both the parent and child for battle. This book is the answer to these

1

prayers! It is a masterfully written prophetic teaching that is both rich in revelation and simple in application.

Small But Mighty rises to answer the needs of parents raising children called of God. Whether you are a parent with young children, a teacher or children's minister, a grandparent, or a loving aunt or uncle, this teaching will help you. It will provide insight to effectively speak into and pray over the destiny of the children that you love!

May the Church push back, with passion and wisdom, the plans and strategies of hell against this next generation! May we win these battles and effectively release a generation into the ripe harvest fields amongst the nations. May we prepare people for the great outpouring for which we are contending.

> *'And it shall be in the last days,' God says, 'That I will pour forth of My Spirit on all mankind; And your sons and your daughters shall prophesy, And your young men shall see visions, And your old men shall dream dreams'* (Acts 2:17).

The Spirit of God has been released upon the generations! The message of the Kingdom of God is going forth globally. I believe the fire of the Spirit of God is being turned up a notch. We are alive in times of unprecedented opportunity and harvest! God is moving amongst every tribe, tongue, and nation. The tsunami is coming! We must be prepared at every age to ride the wave and experience the great move of God!

RYAN LESTRANGE
Author, *60 Days of Unusual*
Founder RLM, TRIBE network and iHubs Movement

2

INTRODUCTION

You may ask why this book and why now? My answer to that question is simple. When school shootings are becoming more and more common, children aged 11-18 are being labeled as killers of each other, child trafficking is increasing, and children are killing themselves because of bullying, I had no choice, I had to do something. I could not sit back and watch another child die.

Hopefully and prayerfully, this book will grab parental attention and will be a tool used to cause an eye-opening catalyst of change in homes all around the world. *Small but Mighty* is a tool parents can use as a resource to better understand the weapons that Heaven biblically provides to all of those honored to raise a "giant killer" on earth.

We need to ask ourselves, *What is happening to our children, and when was their sweet innocence stolen?* In this book I am asking, "Where were the parents of a whole generation while their children's minds were being warped and overtaken by evil imaginations?" If seeing children being trafficked and becoming heartless murderers at epidemic proportions doesn't alarm parents to wake up, I am officially diagnosing them with a disease called "willful blindness."

If you get nothing out of reading this book but the next point, then it was a success:

OUR CHILDREN ARE UNDER ATTACK; BUT PARENTS CAN INTERCEPT THE PLANS OF THE ENEMY IF WE HEED THE ALARMS GOING OFF URGING US TO WAKE UP. WE MAY HAVE LOST SOME BATTLES ALREADY, BUT THERE STILL IS TIME TO WIN THE WAR RAGING AGAINST THEM.

Small but Mighty in its inception could have been titled so many different things such as, Supernatural Parenting or Teach Their Hands to War, but once I was given the name, *Small but Mighty,* I knew it was the perfect summarizing title for this book. Our children may be small in natural statue, but they can be mighty in the spirit. There are no limits to what we have seen young warriors of the Bible do. From Jeremiah to Jehoshaphat, from young David, to the three Hebrew boys, and now your son and your daughter too can be added to the eternally long list of giant killers.

This book has taken me well over ten years to compile. The stories are real, the struggles are real, and the expressed revelations are real. I do not have the market cornered on spiritual warfare or child psychology, but what I do have and plan to share in this book is more than a decade of parenting pitfalls and victories with the hope that you too can learn and overcome.

During one of the scariest times of my life when I was searching all over for a resource to aid and provide spiritual insight on warfare for children—I found there was nothing. My prayer is that this book fills a big gaping void in the area of parenting supernaturally in the 21st century.

Our children are our most valuable gifts. They are our dreams, fulfillment of said dreams, hope, and our future. We invest our time, finances, visions, and whole lives into our children. We are entrusted to guard and protect the innocent beauties that the Father has given us.

There has been an alarm set off in the heavenlies requesting parents to wake up to the fact that their children are under a life- and destiny-altering assault. Once awakened, it's important to know that no matter what part of the journey you may find your- self, there is still hope of restoration and reconciliation in Christ.

I am reminded of so many heart-wrenching conversations over the years with parents discussing the challenges they were facing with their children. From those conversations, I have concluded that the majority of those parents' most frustrating times were when their children came under attack. It's one thing for an adult to go through, but when your children are being preyed upon, there is a higher level of alarm and desperation you feel.

I can attest to this assertion because my greatest moments of unrest were when my son came under spiritual demonic attack. Feeling ill-equipped and helpless only fueled my panic in not knowing how to stop it. As a parent, I know it's my role to protect my children, but not being able to combat what's coming their way is an emotional turbulence that is simply unexplainable and challenging to articulate.

In those seasons of warfare, I was provoked to fervently press into the Word of God, seek counsel, and be still enough to hear from the Holy Spirit on how to shift and move. Out of that season, I gained a righteous indignation toward the works of the enemy and what he tried and still tries to do to our most valuable jewels, our children.

It's this same indignation that propels me to write this book and sound an alarm declaring that it's time to raise up a generation of children who are aware that they are in a war, expose what weapons they have to fight back, and teach them how to no longer be bullied in the spirit realm. Our children are our future. Shouldn't we invest in making sure they are spiritually equipped and emotionally healthy? Shouldn't we make sure that they are well-endowed with the spiritual tools to combat the strategic attacks sent to take them out?

Now more than ever we must hand out tools of effective engagement to dismantle the works of the enemy. The children of this generation are under an all-out assault. Their minds are being overrun with philosophies, hidden dark messages, distractions, doctrines of devils, and perverted ways of living that their hearts and souls are not equipped to refute or process.

WE MUST BE AGGRESSIVE IN TORMENTING THE SAME SYSTEMS THAT FEEL AUTHORIZED TO ATTACK AND POLLUTE THE MINDS OF THIS GENERATION. WE MUST UPROOT AND ANNIHILATE THE DEMONIC SEEDS THAT PURPOSE TO BEAR STRANGE FRUIT IN THE LIVES OF OUR CHILDREN.

The realm of the spirit is real, and many of our children are experiencing demonic daydreams and dark trances that seek to keep them frozen in fear. Consider:

- What if your child is not just "going through a phase"? What if they are under a demonic spiritual undoing?
- What if their rebellious tendencies are being fueled by hellish, ignited frustrations imparted through

an unclosed door in the heart of your child, or even you?

■ What if your child's unusual infatuation with the opposite or same sex is being ignited by the spirit of perversion possibly passed down by the bloodline or something their gates—eyes, ears, touch, smell, sense—have been exposed to?

■ What if their nightmares are being influenced by familiar spirits to cultivate an atmosphere of fear and intimidation in their hearts?

Getting the breakthrough answers to these questions early on are crucial to the spiritual health of your child and allows for a better opportunity to lessen heartaches, detours, and scars in their lives. There are a lot of books on deliverance that are necessary and amazing—but let's get to a place where we are more focused on *early prevention and guarding the lives of our children* to avoid the necessity of demonic deliverance in their lives.

Our children are entrusted to us by God to raise them up in the fear and knowledge of who they are and who the Father is in them. It is our responsibility to empower ourselves and in turn empower them to be able to stand in the midst of adversity and resist the devil to cause him to flee.

Submit yourselves therefore to God. Resist the devil, and he will flee from you (James 4:7 KJV).

It's time to get the tools necessary to send the devil on an eternal marathon run that does not have a finish line. I pray you're ready.

Buckle up, because it's going to be a very empowering ride for you and your child.

Chapter One

RULES OF WARFARE

Mommi, R Ther Rools?

"Sumthin biten me, Mommi, sumthin biten me, come ere!" Fear gripped my heart being awakened by hearing these words from my two-year-old son at three o'clock in the morning. This was night number three; nights one and two were the start of a long journey into the school of spiritual warfare for my family. During that season, sleep had become a thing of the past, a priceless commodity, and something I truly needed.

My exhaustion was exacerbated by being about four months pregnant, and the events that were taking place sent my Type A personality, where things need to add up, swirling. My son had experienced nightmares in the past, but never to the point where he was waking up with actual marks and scratches on his tiny arms—not inflicted by him, of course. This was new to me, overwhelming and extremely scary. It was the horror film people go see for entertainment except this was nowhere close to funny.

I kept thinking of movies I had watched in the past of haunted houses and wondered if that was our present reality. Even exploring

11

this as an option just swung wider the already open door of fear in my life. The facts were: we just moved into this home; never had any issues before; I knew the owners who were God-fearing people so as far as I knew; it wasn't given over to anything dark in nature; besides, even if it was, my husband and I were saved and Spirit-filled Christians, so we should be covered and unable to get attacked like this, right?

What cause does the enemy have to attack a defenseless two-year-old child anyway? What did my son ever do to him? So many questions flooded my mind in an attempt to rationalize what was really happening. I remember thinking, *This is just so unfair! There's got to be rules against this kind of thing; and if there are, where can I find them?*

Still grappling with the idea that this was a spiritual attack, I quickly grabbed the most logical concept I could think of. I remember thinking, *Maybe it's not even the enemy, maybe it's something he ate or some kind of allergic reaction; after all, the devil does get blamed for every little thing anyways.* No matter how much I tried to rationalize what I was seeing and sensing, I knew deep down in my heart that what we were experiencing was not caused by some kind of allergic reaction. An allergic reaction could never create the dark atmosphere I was sensing during those nights or be the cause of the terrified reactions my two-year-old was displaying.

Day Three

Extremely exhausted, I stumbled out of my bed and followed the tiny little finger pointing me to his bedroom for the third night in a row. As I was following my son to his room, his eyes were trying to communicate that there *was* something in there. I have to admit, seeing this wide-eyed two-year-old's fearful anticipation made me even more afraid. I'm the kind of person who literally over-dramatizes almost everything, so the movie screen of my mind was going ballistic.

Growing up, I hated even hearing adults have conversations about demonic activity or casting out demons. Just hearing the stories would almost guarantee a nightmare about what was spoken. Ever since I was little I used to have unwanted dreams that I was casting out demons or waring against them in some capacity. Outside of my dream life, I was never exposed to any natural understanding of this concept, so it was not only foreign but way too over the top for me to handle. I always told myself that was a ministry I would *never* get into.

Little did I know almost fourteen years later I would be writing a book on equipping others on how to combat the works of the enemy in their and their children's lives. This in itself is a revelation because I believe that the enemy gets wind of certain individual's gifts and calls very early on; and if he can sow a seed of fear to detour that ministry, then he assumes, mission accomplished. He forgets that God's Word says, "All things will work out for their good," even the pain of torment.

Those yesteryears are the catalyst that fuels my passion to tell as many people as I can that the enemy is the world's biggest flimflammer! Here's the definition for readers who are like, *Flimflammer? Huh?* Flimflammer: a trick or deception, especially a swindle or confidence game involving skillful persuasion or clever manipulation of the victim. A piece of nonsense; twaddle.

Night Three Continued

Knowing I couldn't abandon the little person I loved so much in his time of need, I mustered up enough strength to go through the same motions that I did on nights one and two. I turned on his room light, looked under his bed, and opened his closet doors just to prove to him that he was having another horrible dream and that nothing was really in his room. I prayed over him, tucked him in, and said good night, again.

Ugh! Day three's events continued to days four, five, six, seven, eight, nine, and finally to night ten! Sometimes the same things would happen two to three times in a night. One night I remember saying good night to him at least four times. I was exacerbated and completely out of options. I was tired beyond explanation and totally felt alone in this fight. I finally came to a place of complete desperation and felt like I needed some help before I went off the deep end.

Teach His Hands to War

As a result of all the stress, lack of sleep, and tears, I remember on day ten crying so hard I got a pounding headache. Has that ever happened to you? In the middle of this pity party and having no more tears to cry, I remember sitting there simply quiet. I was quiet long enough to hear a voice, a still small one, whispering, "Why are you lying to him?"

Huh? Yup, that was my reaction. Then I thought, *Wait, after all these days of torment, that's the most comforting thing You can think of to say to me?* Like a good Father, He wasn't pulled into my tantrum, He proceeded as if I never lashed out, and said very simply, "There *is* something in his room."

"God, what do You want me to do, tell my two-year-old son that there *are* monsters in his room?"

"No! Teach his hands to war," was God's response. I think my whole body shuttered hearing those words. It felt as if time stood still at that very moment.

Blessed be the Lord, my Rock, who trains my hands for war, and my fingers for battle (Psalm 144:1 NKJV).

You may be cheering and clapping, or perhaps this scene may remind you of a good scene from a movie you watched, but that was *NOT* my reaction. I was so angry, "WAR? Lord," I screamed, "I thought *You* fight our battles. Why don't you send Gabriel, Michael, or some other archangel to help us get rid of this thing attacking my child?"

I never felt so alone and ill-equipped to fight anything as I did that night. How can I teach something to my child I myself didn't understand? Furthermore, how do you teach a two-year-old to fight and stand against an invisible monster that only saw fit to visit us in the middle of the night. Such a coward it was!

Do Not Disturb, Class in Session

Being taught in the middle of the battle most definitely raised my level of attentiveness and eagerness for the instruction. I remembered asking the Lord for the words to say, my response after picking myself up off the floor was, "OK, if You give me the words say, I will surely say them, but pleaseeee just teach me, so I can teach him."

That night my spiritual warfare training commenced. We had a long road ahead of us; but to know that help was on the way gave me a spark of hope that my soul desperately longed for.

Immediately after this conversation, I remembered purchasing a book a few months previously by well-known author Cindy Trimm, titled *The Rules of Engagement.* I hadn't started to read it yet, but at that moment I felt like I needed to find it and read it. So I got up from the floor, grabbed the little book, and began reading out loud while walking the halls of my house. In and out of my son's room I walked quoting the spiritual warfare prayers written on the pages of that small but mighty prayer manual.

I must have read those prayers for hours; first very quietly, scared, and timid. I was still afraid because I didn't feel like I was walking those halls alone. I sensed a large, eerie presence hovering around. My overactive imagination didn't help either by painting images of ugly things jumping out at me. All of this was new and oh so strange, but being a determined person by nature, I would not quit that night. I felt like I was on the verge of victory and knew for the sake of my son, I had to continue until there was peace.

Only God's twins, grace and mercy, got me through those nights. I constantly reminded myself of the Scripture where God declared that He would never leave us nor forsake us.

> *Be strong and courageous. Do not be afraid or terrified because of them, for the Lord your God goes with you; he will never leave you nor forsake you* (Deuteronomy 31:6 NIV).

I wrapped my mind around these words until the greatest presence in my life was no longer fear and torment but rather peace and the loving arms of my Father.

Victory and Stillness

After hours of praying and declaring, I remember suddenly feeling a quiet peace, then a stillness evaded the room. It was finally still enough for me to go lay down and try to sleep. The next time I opened my eyes my two-year-old son was standing over me asking for something to eat.

Yes! It was morning and we made it through the night: Victory #1.

The battle was on after that night. I can't tell you the night terror did not come back; it did, but when it did, I was better prepared. Through those attacks, I learned how to pray on another level, declare the Word of the Lord, and teach my son that he had a host of heavenly help ready to be deployed on his behalf. During that season he learned the following two Scripture verses that just so happen to be two of his favorite Scriptures that he still quotes to this day:

> *No weapon formed against me shall prosper and every word that rises up against me I shall condemn* (Isaiah 54:17, paraphrased).
> *God has not given us [me] the spirit of fear, but of power and of love and a sound mind* (2 Timothy 1:7 NKJV).

My prayers turned from "God, what is happening? Lord help me!" To, "Satan, I bind you and every demonic force that is attacking my child and home. You have no legal right or authority in our home, and I command you to go in the powerful name of Jesus Christ!"

Even though we claimed victory over that particular terror, somewhere within me I knew there were more battles to come. From that point on, I began educating myself on spiritual warfare and how to strategically fight the enemy to ensure constant victory.

By no means am I professing to be a spiritual warfare expert or want to portray that my story is the only way to defeat the enemy. It is fourteen years later, and I am still learning new weapons of warfare. It's been an amazing journey and have learned through biblical studies coupled with life experiences that as children of the Most High God, we have the authority to overcome every attack of the enemy that tries to infiltrate our lives.

I believe the Holy Spirit has prompted me to write this book for parents, grandparents, aunts, uncles, and any relative or guardian who was or is in the same position I was in when my son was two years old. As a parent or guardian, this book will give you understanding of spiritual warfare in a practical manner. This book will get you to a place where you are not making comments like the following regarding spiritual warfare, "Well maybe she/he should not have eaten that pizza after eight o'clock."

There's nothing worse than being attacked yourself, but another level of panic comes when one of your children is suffering. We owe it to ourselves and our children to learn how to combat the enemy for not if he comes, but when he comes. The Word says that the enemy's purpose is to *"steal, kill, and destroy"* (John 10:10). He is literally prowling around, seeking people to devour (1 Peter 5:8) including our children. The enemy does not care about the age of our children. If he can attack them while they are young and even in the womb, which we will talk about later, he most definitely will.

The enemy's job is to prevent children from focusing on God's love and purposes for them, to steal their destinies, and to potentially avoid getting his tail kicked later on in their adult life. The next time he comes to attack you or yours, you must be equipped and prepared for battle. You would never show up to a gunfight, gun-less, would you? Why do saints feel it is OK to live our lives without understanding our weapons of warfare—yet still expect to overcome?

The time of not knowing is over!

*Put on all of God's armor so that you will be able to stand firm against all strategies of the devil. For we are not fighting against flesh-and-blood enemies, but against evil rulers and authorities of the unseen world, against mighty powers in this dark world, and against evil spirits in the heavenly places. Therefore, put on every piece of God's armor so you will be able to resist the enemy in the time of evil. Then after the battle you will still be standing firm. Stand your ground, putting on the **belt of truth** and the body armor of God's righteousness. For **shoes, put on the peace** that comes from the Good News so that you will be fully prepared. In addition to all of these, hold up the **shield of faith** to stop the fiery arrows of the devil. Put on **salvation as your helmet**, and take the **sword of the Spirit**, which is the word of God. **Pray in the Spirit** at all times and on every occasion. Stay alert and be persistent in your*

19

prayers for all believers everywhere (Ephesians 6:11-18 NLT).

Nine times out of ten when someone mentions the words "spiritual warfare," Ephesians 6 will shortly be quoted afterward. I love to look at the Word of God as a diary heirloom handed down to generation after generation detailing eternal strategies on how to win daily. The Bible is very clear that if we do not put on the armor of God, we will not be able to stand firm against the wiles of the devil. There is no way around it, we must learn every piece of armor so well that putting it on becomes like second nature.

Teaching your children these spiritual concepts can be challenging, especially if they are younger, but every day is an opportunity for you to reinforce these concepts in their lives. The park, the home, and the car are all classrooms. The idea is to constantly look for opportunities to share lessons that can be taught to your child during their everyday lives.

But first things first. In order to educate your child on how the armor can be used, you yourself must fully understand and implement it in your own life.

My first instruction before engaging is to make sure that you don't have any holes in your armor. Make sure your weapons are effective, and that the lines in the war in which you fight are clearly drawn. In other words, there should be no question that you are a child of God. The enemy's accusation against you should not be that you partied and slept with him last night. The lines in the sand need to be clear-cut; fighting a war with holes in your armor is a fixed fight in the wrong direction. You don't want to do that.

You want your prayers and declarations honored in Heaven and obeyed in hell. You don't want to be praying a prayer commanding the devil to flee and he laughs at you while filing his nails. Please understand what I'm saying, we all have sinned and come short of the glory of God, but once we have confessed with our mouths and believed in our hearts that Jesus Christ is Lord and He arose on the third day, we are washed by the blood of Christ and saved. At that point we are set on the journey of working out our own salvation, but holiness is still Heaven's standard (Philippians 2:12). And by the grace of God, every day is a day for you as a leader in your home to demonstrate what godliness looks like.

The enemy loves to take advantage of believers who forget whose child they really are. Living a life of total surrender to God and walking in the way His Word instructs gives us a badge of holiness and obedience that is one of the most effective weapons we can use. Obedience is a key ingredient in the fuel that ignites our prayers and sets them on fire.

I Learned by Watching You, OK?

I don't think I can ever forget the commercial where the parent was trying to scold the child for smoking, and the parent yelled at the child saying, "Where did you learn that!?" And the child said, "I learned it by watching you." Studies show children do more of what they see their parents do rather than what the parents say. Understanding this concept gives you an advantage because you don't always have to be verbally teaching. Your children watch you very closely, they watch to see how you handle pressure, stress, and trials. How you get through more than likely will be their same strategy on how to make it through as well. Let's commit to making sure that we are modeling behaviors we would not mind our children mirroring.

I encourage you to allow your child to join your spiritual journey with the Father. While you yourself are worshipping, let your child join in. Demonstration is a very powerful tool that allows your child to not only be told what to do but is shown how it actually works in real life.

OK, back to Ephesians 6:

> **Put on all of God's armor** so that you will be able to **stand firm** against all strategies of the devil (Ephesians 6:11 NLT).

Wow, I Have My Own Armor!

No weapon anyone can ever create will measure up to the spiritual devices of the enemy as being effective. Like Ephesians says, you cannot fight a spiritual realm with natural resources. That would be like using a real baseball bat to hit an invisible baseball that only exists in your imagination. I know, sounds ludicrous, right?

OK, now let's dig into these spiritual weapons discussed in Ephesians called the armor of God by breaking each one down according to the function in our lives as citizens of the Kingdom of God. These weapons will help you and your child stand against any onslaught of attacks that the enemy has already planned for you.

It's an interesting point to highlight that all weapons but the sword are non-offensive weapons dealing with matters of the heart condition versus yielding or pursuing weapons. This point is major because much of the warfare is standing on the truths of God's Word, knowing you are victorious, having faith you will make it through, being unmovable, unshakeable in times of gross pressure, holding onto the promises of God and His truths is a summarization of the functions of the weapons that make up this spiritual armor of God.

Where's My Belt?

*Stand your ground, putting on the **belt of truth** and the body armor of God's righteousness* (Ephesians 6:14 NLT).

Why start with a belt? The Bible was written during a time when the Roman soldiers wore very specific garments in strategic ways. Studies show that the belt was such a major piece of the armor, that if forgotten, the soldier would not have a place to hang his sword. I never forgot the message I heard about facts versus truth. During seasons of great hardship and the facts staring at us paint a convincing picture of defeat, we have to remind ourselves as believers that we do not stand on the facts—we stand on what is truth. Fact may be you feel defeated; but the truth is, you are victorious. A fact could be that the doctor diagnosed you with a sickness; but the truth is, healing is the children's bread (Matthew 15:22-28). The fact could be you do not see how your child's behavior could ever turn around, but the truth is, all things are possible through Christ (Matthew 19:26; Luke 1:37; Mark 9:23; Mark 10:27 KJV).

Parents have to also understand that truth is not self-dictated but mandated by our heavenly Father. I hear all the time people saying, "It's OK if it's your truth." "Just tell your truth;" but the reality of that statement is one person's truth may not be truth at all, but simply that person's perspective about some facts.

Parent, we have to teach our children the God-breathed principles in the Word of God and then measure our facts or our truth up against that. Anything else could open a door and allow destructive outcomes that pollute our lives and the lives of our children in ways that healing will be imminent.

Telling the truth, believing the truth, living the truth, not lying to get out of trouble, and allowing the integrity of your life to be held up by the belt of truth is a weapon.

Sharing this concept with your child could sound a little like this...

> Hi, _____ (insert child's name). I want to share with you the ways you can live that makes you a winner. God loves it when we are honest and truthful. He also wants us to believe what He says about us. Remember when we talked about the armor of God (assuming this topic is not new), well every day when you wake up, you have to say to yourself, *I will tell the truth today, and I will believe what God says about me. I'm a great kid and I know He loves me,* and doing that shows God that you are putting on the belt of truth. Did you put on your belt today?

You can even ask your children, when you think they're not being honest, "Do you have your belt of truth on?" This is a practical way to teach and remind them how to respond using this particular piece of armor. This question should not be used as a form of condemnation, rather as a reminder and a tool of self-awareness.

*Make them holy by **your** [God's] truth; teach them **your** word, which is **truth*** (John 17:17 NLT).

A Plate on My Chest?

*Stand firm then, with the belt of truth buckled around your waist, with the **breastplate of righteousness** in place* (Ephesians 6:14 NIV).

Isaiah 59:17 (NASB) is a prophetic declaration of how Jesus was to conquer and win, *"He put on righteousness like a breastplate."*

I am not surprised that the writer of Ephesians, apostle Paul, was able to see way back into the Book of Isaiah and connect Jesus's victories to how He walked and the statutes He so graciously upheld. Righteousness, simply put, is walking as Christ would, living out of the mind and character of God.

A weapon against the enemy is right living and right thinking. In today's culture and time, deciding what is right for some can be a little unclear, especially when you have laws mandating biblical abominations. *Realizing this, we cannot allow for our morality to be mandated by cultural worldviews.*

Our measuring stick of what's "right" is the Word of God—and anything contradictory is a lying deception. The breastplate is the part of armor that protects the heart, and the heart houses our deepest desires, ways, and affections. If we can daily align our hearts with God's, we then are putting on the breastplate of righteousness. The goal is to have our hearts abundantly overflowing with what's in God's heart.

Similar to the belt of truth, because they go hand in hand, the breastplate of righteousness is a weapon strengthened by how we think and live. All of the weapons are interconnected and work together, but the belt and breastplate connect to matters of the heart.

It's hard to walk uprightly when your heart doesn't have the desire to do so. As a parent, it's important to understand what's going on in the heart of your child. What are their motivations? What is important to them? Are there any underlying motivations rooted by wayward thinking that need to be uprooted? It is very important to teach your child that it really does pay to live right.

> *The Lord has rewarded me according to my righteousness; according to the cleanness of my hands He has recompensed* [rewarded] *me* (Psalm 18:20 NASB).

A reinforcing activity could be to do just that. When your children respond according to having their breastplate in place, affirm and reward them with kind words to reinforce God's character in them.

Shoes of Peace

> *For shoes, put on the peace that comes from the Good News so that you will be fully prepared* (Ephesians 6:15 NLT).

Wearing these shoes as part of your armor ensures peace. Peace in the heart of your child is a weapon. This portion of Scripture teaches your child that God truly does want them to live in peace. The New King James Version says, *"and having shod your feet with the preparation of the gospel of peace...."* To have their feet "shod" to peace is to have their feet anchored to the good news of peace. Peace can be explained as the absence of fear and disturbance. I would like to add that true peace is knowing God's got my back even in the middle of a hard time. This can only be secured with the understanding that because God is peace and we are His, we have the right to live in peace.

Peace is the assurance that it's all going to work out. Peace is soundness of mind, not doubleminded and riddled with confusion. There is peace available even in the middle of a warfare storm. Jesus demonstrated this very well as He slept while the boat rocked away in the middle of a thundering rain storm. Though Jesus was with His disciples, they failed to allow for peace to be the greater reality at that time. (See Mark 4:35-41.)

This is a major lesson that all parents can learn and teach their children—choosing what to allow to master our hearts and minds, peace or the storm. Though everyone faces situations that may vary in intensity and hardship, we always have the option to choose the Gospel of peace.

How can this translate to your child? I would say very carefully. Children are still in their own journey of learning how to handle stress and things that come to "undo them." Each instance is an opportunity for you share that even while they are figuring it out, God doesn't want them to be riddled with anxiety and torment because of it. *Teaching them to trust God in tough times is one of the most important lessons they will ever learn in life.* I am always looking for examples to highlight and show my children that God cares for them and cares for everything concerning them.

Casting all your care on Him, for He cares for you (1 Peter 5:7 NKJV).

My daughter for weeks kept asking for a specific water bottle; being only seven at the time, this was a major request, as "all the other kids" in her class either had a water bottle or one like the one she really wanted. Don't get me wrong, I wanted her to have a water bottle too, but it was not high on the agenda of items on my to-do list.

One Saturday she asked me for it and I purposed in my heart that this was going to be the day that I was going to go shopping to get it. After looking at a few stores, we either could not find the one she wanted or the ones we found were way above the price I was willing to spend for a water bottle. Since it was getting late, I told her we would have to try again the next day. This sent her little seven-year-old emotions into a hurricane, tears of frustration flooded her little face, and not having this one thing simply ruined her night.

Later that evening we were attending my nephew's one-year-old birthday party at my sister's home. As soon as Moriah stepped in their home, everyone could see that she was just not herself. Her uncle very kindly asked her, "Moriah, what's wrong, what's going on?" Moriah began to explain her trial through tears of frustration. Her uncle said, "You know what, Moriah, I think we may actually have that same water bottle that you have been wanting." He grabbed her hand and said, "Let's go take a look." Not even five minutes later, Moriah comes out of the kitchen beaming and holding the same sparkly blue water bottle that fit the very description of what she was asking for.

The first thing that came out of my mouth, because I am always in teacher mode, was, "Wow, Moriah, God knew you really wanted that water bottle and He really cares about even the small things. You should thank God for loving you so well." Beaming ear to ear she said, "Mom, I already did."

I take every chance I get to demonstrate God's faithful kindness in practical ways to her so that she has her own testimonial journey that it will all work out—not just because her mother said so but now she has testimonies of her own to stand on. It is crucial that your children are taught to have their own relationship with their heavenly Father that is not hinged upon yours, because relationship with God is a weapon.

Faith is a Shield

*In addition to all of these, hold up the **shield of faith** to stop the fiery arrows of the devil* (Ephesians 6:16 NLT).

The shield of faith distinguishes the fiery arrows that fly by day at us. This weapon is one that truly does please God when we wear it. The Bible teaches us that it is impossible to please God without faith. Our whole relationship with God is hinged upon us believing He is who He says He is and He can do what He says He can do. Not believing one of those two truths creates a fracture in our relationship with God that cannot be repaired until we have the "faith" to believe God never lies. Without faith—the ability to see the possible in impossible circumstances; or the ability to see and believe without natural proof—we cannot, like a child, take the Father at His Word, which is a punch, coupled with a slap in His face.

Why Is Faith Associated with a Shield?

The enemy will throw fiery darts at us because that's his job. The shield of faith is a weapon that helps us deflect evil darts and render them useless. The shield was the largest part of the Roman soldier's armor. It was large enough to hide behind; yet like the sword is a weapon you have to pick up and actually decide to strategically use. Daniel being thrown into the lion's den; David killing Goliath; Noah building the ark; Abraham leaving his home and journeying into new a land—they all required faith to believe for the next big, unknown life experience.

Do not think for one moment that each of those spiritual warriors were not met with an onslaught of fiery darts (accusations; or any thought that is opposite to God's) by the enemy trying to get them to abandon their missions. Just like those fathers of faith, we too should expect the fiery darts. But by wielding our shield of faith, we are assured of a victory every time we use it.

THE OPPOSITE OF FAITH IS DOUBT.

The Scriptures teach us that we are all born with *"a measure of faith"* (Romans 12:3 NKJV) and it also says, *"Faith comes by hearing, and hearing by the word of God"* (Romans 10:17 NKJV). Our faith can be increased the more we allow God's Word to be heard in our lives. It's crucial for your children to be surrounded by the Word of God. There is never too much—the Word is living and brings life to your child's heart. Even when you think they are not paying attention, their spirits are drinking in the words of life that will rage war against any work that seeks to come against them.

Faith can be fed and increased; if not fed, it will starve and become dismantled by doubt.

What doubts do your children have connecting to this whole Jesus thing? What doubts do your children have about God and how much He loves them? This is a great time to ask! Begin to teach your child that *doubt is a fiery dart* sent to dismantle the stronghold of truth in their lives. Doubt can be a cancer, so discovering it while they're young and distinguishing it together with the Holy Spirit is a powerful weapon against the plans of the enemy.

Don't Ride Without a Helmet

*Put on salvation as your **helmet**...* (Ephesians 6:17 NLT).

I'm sure you tell your children to wear their helmets when they want to ride their bikes. So, this weapon will not be hard to explain because helmets, unlike swords, are used and seen in our everyday lives. Either they have worn one, or they have seen plenty of other people wearing helmets.

The question is, why would the helmet be coupled with salvation? What does salvation have to do with a helmet? This question is very understandable; but once you fundamentally understand salvation, you will clearly be able to see the correlation and explain it to your children.

Salvation is defined as the act of being "saved" or delivered from death. To deeper our understanding of salvation, I believe it warrants the discovery of what are we being saved from? I honestly did not ask that question until twenty years after being saved, receiving salvation. I always assumed I was saved just so I would not go to hell; when in all actuality, not going to hell is simply the by-product of salvation. I know this could appear to be a play on words, but stay with me.

The Bible teaches us that the payment or by-product of sin is death, *"the wages of sin is death"* (Romans 6:23 NKJV). When you do a word study, you will quickly find that "sin" is any thought, action, or deed that is opposite to God's. You will also discover that there are two deaths described in the Bible—a natural death and a spiritual death. I would like to interject that though natural deaths can occur because of sinful ways, this Scripture is also speaking of spiritual death and separation from God.

When our minds become ill and diseased with sin, we are in need of the Savior, Jesus Christ. The only One who can reconcile us back to the thoughts and ways of our Father. The Bible teaches us that God did just that—He sent His Son Jesus to redeem us to our rightful place. Jesus became a curse to break ours; He became sin so that He could overcome ours. There is no temptation known to humankind that Jesus did not handle on the Cross.

Acknowledging while believing in our hearts unto confession is the act of being saved (Romans 10:9).

Our choice to believe in Christ and what He did for us is a conscious decision that is manufactured and determined in our minds; so if we can put a helmet of protection around that every day, we then are putting on the helmet of salvation. The helmet is yet another weapon that protects our way of thinking, which should be God's way of thinking. Not allowing the enemy or the culture of this world to infiltrate the beliefs that mirror God's means putting on the helmet of salvation daily.

One resounding idea you will hear echoed throughout this book is the importance of "God thinking." The way we think is so important to God that at one point in time He destroyed everything on the whole earth because of the way people thought. As a parent, another life lesson to teach your child is to discipline themselves in the area of God-like thinking, it truly is a WWJD (What would Jesus Do) lifestyle.

> *The Lord observed the extent of human wickedness on the earth, and he saw that **everything they thought or imagined was consistently and totally evil**. So the Lord was sorry he had ever made them and put them on the earth. It broke his heart. And the Lord said, "I will wipe this human race I have created from the face of the earth. Yes, and I will destroy every living thing—all the people, the large animals, the small animals that scurry along the ground, and even the birds of the sky. I am sorry I ever made them"* (Genesis 6:5-7 NLT).

Mid-Chapter Exercise: Flash Card Mania

Casting down imaginations, and every high thing that exalteth itself against the knowledge of God, and bringing into captivity every thought to the obedience of Christ (2 Corinthians 10:5 KJV).

The following is a suggested game that can be used to train your child on how to identify and destroy thoughts that war against the knowledge of who God is and who He is in them (2 Corinthians 10:6).

On about 20 small pieces of paper, write one sentence on each. Some describing a "God thought" and others describing how the enemy thinks. The following are a few examples that can be used as templates. Teach your child how to destroy enemy thoughts by replacing them with God thoughts.

God thought examples:

- Susie looks sad today, I think I'll sit with her at lunch.
- It looks like Jake doesn't have any clothes that fit. I'm going to ask Mom if we can give him some of my nice clothes that are too small for me.
- Melissa doesn't have any gloves, I think I'll give her mine.
- My brother really bothers me, but I'm going to love him anyway.

Enemy thought examples:

- Tim has a hole in his shoe, I am going to tell everyone in the classroom he's poor.

- Robert doesn't have any lunch. I think I'll eat mine in front of him without sharing.
- Mom asked if I did my chores. I'm too tired, so I'll just tell her I did.
- Dad told me to say I'm sorry to my sister, but I'm not going to.

The Spirit's Sword

*...and take the **sword of the Spirit,** which is the word of God* (Ephesians 6:17 NLT).

The sword is the only part of the armor that is described and used in an offensive way. The sword is used by soldiers to harm and to kill their opponent. From a spiritual standpoint, the sword is the written and divinely spoken Word of God. The sword that Paul writes about during his time was the "gladius sword," which during that culture was known as the "sword that conquered the world." Deriving from Spanish developers, this particular sword, like the Word of God, was double edged. It was a formidable tool used in the hands of Roman soldiers that would even pierce through metal.

The Word of God is so powerful that God attributes His own word with the same authority level of His name and character. In other Words, standing on God's Word is a sure thing, because His character has been proven that it cannot fail us.

Knowing what "thus sayeth the Lord" for anything situation is a lamp for our feet to see where we are going (Psalm 119:105). Knowing the Bible, the written Word of God is a powerful weapon, declaring the Word of God is a life-saving weapon, memorizing the Word of God is a sustaining weapon, and listening to the Word of God spoken to us is a vital weapon.

A Call to Action

Over the next several weeks, months, and even years, regularly pick a Scripture verse or two that you as a family can memorize together. Some things to make it fun are to offer prizes to those who accomplished the goal. Children are sponges; and with the right motivation and understanding, memorizing Scripture verses can be a very rewarding adventure.

Let's GPS the Battlefield

Understanding our weapons is oh so major; but knowing where the battle takes place is crucial. Not fully comprehending the setting of the war could be the downfall of any spiritual warrior. From medieval times to modern times, scouts are first sent to survey the land. Their goal is to figure out what obstacles could be a hindrances to attacking the opponent and better understand how the battlefield could play in their favor.

Spiritual warfare means we are not in hand-to-hand combat—we are in a spiritual war with unseen adversaries. God desires to take over our minds with His thoughts, His ways, His desires, and His principles. Unfortunately, the same place God desires to take over is desired by the enemy. You need to know that the battlefield really is in our minds.

Instead of the playground, the enemy says, "Meet me in your mind at three o'clock sharp!" Joyce Meyer has done an amazing job exposing where the spiritual battlefield is, and I definitely recommend her books titled, *Battlefield of the Mind, Battlefield of the Mind for Teens,* and *Battlefield of the Mind for Kids,* depending on the age of your children.

I cannot close out this chapter without exposing that our mind is where spiritual warfare happens. I am constantly sharing with my kids, especially after they have had a bad day, the importance of "thinking about what they are thinking about." Scriptures over and over compel us to *"Fix your thoughts on what is true, and honorable, and right, and pure, and lovely, and admirable. Think about things that are excellent and worthy of praise"* (Philippians 4:8 NLT). And, *"Let this mind be in you which was also in Christ Jesus"* (Philippians 2:5 NKJV), not because the author had nothing else to write about but more because they understood the magnitude of auditing our thoughts, as they dictate the outcome of our lives. *"For as he thinks within himself, so is he"* (Proverbs 23:7 The Passion Translation).

Knowing we are in a continuous war with the enemy and his servants of darkness, we must understand the tools that our heavenly Father has given us. The time of not knowing is over.

Hosea 4:6 (NKJV) tells us, *"My people are destroyed for lack of knowledge. Because you have rejected knowledge."*

I do believe this is the season God is exposing spiritual weapons of warfare and raising up many who are willing to share their battles, wars, wins, and losses so that others will not have to repeat the same mistakes. It is very important to understand that empowering yourself and your child with weapons of warfare does not automatically give you a pass from going through challenges and being attacked. The Bible teaches that we *will* have trials and tribulations in this world, but be of good cheer because Christ has overcome them all (John 16:33).

Though the hard times we go through do not feel good, it's because of them that we are stretched, trained, made to rely on God, and circumcised completely and deeply inside. Getting your children to better understand this early on gives them a major tool and understanding that though they have a target on their back and are in a war, they are fighting a fixed fight in their favor and will be victorious.

I pray you're ready for what's next. If you are, buckle up because this journey you are about to embark on is going to be a very empowering ride to greater levels of victory for you and your child.

Points to Ponder

- Fear is a device the enemy uses to make him appear bigger than he really is.
- It's your job to teach and train your child.
- No weapon formed against you will prosper.
- Children can be taught how to stand against evil and for the Lord.
- There are rules, and you have spiritual armor to help you and your child stand.
- The spiritual battlefield is in the mind.

Prayer Declaration

Declare: Lord, I declare under the authority of Jesus Christ that as I embark on this journey of better understanding Your mind and Your word on how to combat the works of the enemy in the life of my child, _____ (insert child's name), that we are covered by the blood of the Lamb and hidden under the shadow of Your wings. I declare that You are our refuge and fortress; and as we are hidden in You, there is no fear or torment allowed.

I declare we are delivered from the hands of the enemy and whatever he does will not prosper against us. Because I dwell in the secret place, the shelter of the Most High, I will find rest under the shadow of the Almighty—whose power no foe can withstand. Lord, I say, You are my refuge and my fortress, my God; on You I lean and rely, and on You I confidently trust. Thank You, God, for You will deliver me from every trap and protect me from deadly disease (Psalm 91:1-3 NLT). *In Jesus's name I pray, amen.*

Scripture Memory Time

But you belong to God, my dear children. You have already won a victory over those people, because the Spirit who lives in you is greater than the spirit who lives in the world (1 John 4:4 NLT).

Have your child write this verse:

_____

_____

_____

_____

_____

_____

_____

Chapter Activation: What Armor?

To reinforce some of the lessons taught in this chapter about the armor of God, ask your children scenario-based questions to match to each piece of armor. Be creative when coming up with scenarios, even use real ones that happen throughout the day.

*Lucy thought she was going to get in trouble for not doing her homework, so when her mom asked her if she finished her homework, Lucy said, "Yes," and lied.

What piece of armor did Lucy forget to put on?

_____

_____

_____

*Charles is having a hard time with believing Jesus Christ is real.

What piece of armor can Charles put on to keep from doubting?

_____

_____

_____

*Tina was bullied today in school when another student said to her, "You're so ugly." Tina responded, "No I'm not. I'm fearfully and wonderfully made."

What piece of armor did Tina use?

_____

_____

_____

*Bobby has been so worried and stressed out because of a test in school. It's all he can think about.

What piece of armor did Bobby forget to put on?

_____

_____

_____

*Marsha doesn't have the desire to do the right thing. She feels her heart has been broken too many times to think about being kind to others.

What piece of armor did Marsha forget to put on?

_____

_____

_____

Congratulations, you are now a spiritual warfare instructor! And your children are on a path toward victory!

Chapter Two

THE KINGDOM OF DARKNESS MADE SIMPLE

We wrestle not against flesh and blood, but against principalities, against powers, against the rulers of the darkness of this world, against spiritual wickedness in high places (Ephesians 6:12 KJV).

Seeing into another realm to some may feel more like a curse; but with training and understanding, this amazing gift can be a tool used to snatch many from darkness and bring them into God's heavenly light. God desires to use the spiritual gifts given to us as vehicles of redemption.

It's very important to know that the invisible enemies we are fighting are real; they are more real than the pages in this book and the tangible things you can see with your eyes.

The Unseen Controls the Seen

Many live out their everyday lives with the illusion that the natural controls the spiritual, when in all actuality it's the spiritual that controls the natural. This may be a new concept for you, so let me restate it using our imaginations as the example. I'm sure you would agree that our imaginations are real, but very much invisible. Before anything can be created, it first must be imagined or thought of in our minds. The imagination of our Creator God is where this creation first lived.

Once a creator begins to build the idea that was imagined, it now can be realized in the natural for others to see and interact with. The reality is that the creation already existed in the realm of the spirit—mind, day dream, dreams, thoughts, unseen realm—first, and then was manifested into the natural, not in the reverse order.

Why is this important? It is important because though you may not see something with your natural eyes does not necessarily mean it is nonexistent. Getting your children to understand this concept is a great start to being victorious when on the battlefield. There is a cool activation at the end of this chapter to assist your child to further understand this concept; but in the meantime, let's see if this next analogy helps to reinforce the point.

Dressed and Ready for War

Picture yourself as a soldier in the US Army. You are dressed in your finest uniform, boots shined, gun fully loaded, and you have been trained by the best of the best. Today is the first day for war against your skillfully trained enemy. The day of dread has come and finally you are being dropped off at the battlefield along with your compatriots. You are pumped and ready for war! Oh, I almost forgot, there is just one more thing, the lieutenant in charge instructs you and the other soldiers to put on blindfolds.

Now, how do you feel?

As a child of God, this is your reality every day. The enemy stealthily seeks you, studies you, and waits for an open door of access to jump you, even while you sleep.

> *Stay alert! Watch out for your great enemy, the devil. He prowls around like a roaring lion, looking for someone to devour* (1 Peter 5:8 NLT).

Do I have your attention now? Like me, you may be saying to yourself, *How is that fair? No one can fight blindfolded.* This revelation may appear to be a mismatched fight. Here is a question to assist in exposing the cracks in that line of thinking. If God loves you, and He does, why would any good father allow you to fight an enemy you can't see and have no chance of defeating? Though I get it, this thought process is a false perception of our loving Father who is perfect in every way.

Let's pray about this: "Lord, change my filters. Father, expose any false perceptions of You that are lies and do not line up with who You truly are. Dismantle the filters that say You are not for me and that You're not a good Father. Amen."

You must trust that the One who created you and cares for you would never put you in a war you could never win. In fact, it's quite the opposite, we are in a fixed fight to our advantage.

> *Yet in all these things we are more than conquerors through Him who loved us* (Romans 8:37 NKJV).

We are more than conquerors through and because of Jesus. The complete work of the Cross was just that, complete. So much happened when Christ Jesus said, "It is finished." It will take us a lifetime to truly uncover all of "it," but one thing we know for sure is that Jesus placed the enemy under His and our feet. The enemy was and will forever be a defeated foe. This is something I love to remind him of every chance I get.

A Little Lower Than Angels

Scriptures esteem God's children—you and me—so highly that He doesn't even recognize the seen human as the enemy, but proclaim that the rulers and the head demons in charge are the ones we wrestle.

> *What is man that You are mindful of him, and the son of man that You visit him? For You have made him a little lower than the angels, and You have crowned him with glory and honor. You have made him to have dominion over the works of Your hands; You have put all **things under his feet*** (Psalm 8:4-6 NKJV).

Congratulations, you're on the varsity wrestling team!

I find it very interesting that the Bible likens our spiritual battles to a wrestling match. I just love the analogies of Heaven used to assist us to fully understand.

One definition of a wrestling match is a fight between two individuals involving gripping and pushing, using special moves and holds to force the opponent onto a mat to a place of surrender.

Ultimately, the goal is to bring your opponent to a place of submission and surrender.

The challenge I see existing today in the church is believers walking around acting like they are defeated and living in a surrendered place. Surrendering to God is necessary; but surrendering to the enemy is unwarranted and a sure sign of not knowing who you are and who you belong to.

Back to the Wrestling Match

To wrestle with powers, rules, and principalities means they must get up close and personal. Yes, that means intrude into your space, place, and home—if permitted. I say "if permitted" because there are rules of engagement, which we will discuss later on.

> *The temptations in your life are no different from what others experience. And God is faithful. He will not allow the temptation to be more than you can stand. When you are tempted, he will show you a way out so that you can endure* (1 Corinthians 10:13 NLT).

First Corinthians 10:13 teaches us that God will not put more on us than we can bear. Even when we feel we are at our wit's end, God knows our breaking capacity and builds us up to become supported, stretched, and strengthened all at the same time.

For God to allow us to have opponents that are rulers says this is a fair match up—both sides are heavyweights. All the wealth of Heaven dwells inside you; so through Christ, we are more than capable of handling our adversaries. How awesome are you to be able to overcome an invisible, trained infantry that has thousands of years of experience engaging and attacking the children of God! The rulers are banking on us remaining ignorant of the fact that we too are rulers and just like them can make commands and expect results.

Lucifer's Eviction

How you are fallen from heaven, O Lucifer, son of the morning! How you are cut down to the ground, you who weakened the nations! For you have said in your heart: "I will ascend into heaven, I will exalt my throne above the stars of God; I will also sit on the mount of the congregation on the farthest sides of the north; I will ascend above the heights of the clouds, I will be like the Most High." Yet you shall be brought down to Sheol, to the lowest depths of the Pit. Those who see you will gaze at you, and consider you, saying: "Is this the man who made the earth tremble, who shook kingdoms, who made the world as a wilderness and destroyed its cities, who did not open the house of his prisoners?" (Isaiah 14:12-17 NKJV)

From this Scripture passage in Isaiah 14, we can conclude that the unveiling of satan is going to be a pretty pathetic and disappointing event, one where you probably would demand to get your money back. Since the enemy's eviction from heavenly places, he uses whatever tricks he can to promote fear in our hearts toward him in an effort to appear stronger than the One who is greater in us. The Bible clearly states that greater is our God in us than he that is in the world. *"You belong to God, my dear children. You have already won a victory over those people, because the Spirit who lives in you is greater than the spirit who lives in the world"* (1 John 4:4 NLT). So why do we continue to fall for the enemy's illusions and continue to believe his lies?

48

I Look Like My Daddy

Like the Godhead—Father, Son, Holy Spirit—we are made up of three parts—spirit, soul, and body—that encompasses the all of who we are. But the real essence of who we are is spirit, like our Father. We are a spirit housed in a body of flesh and bones that has a soul. We also have God-like abilities; and as sons and daughters, we walk in and carry His authority.

Don't be alarmed at the attacks and battles you may face; for our anointing, which is our God-given ability to fight the adversary, grows by the number of battles we fight and ultimately win. When you overcome, you gain authority over what you overcame and now have legal right to assist with dismantling such in the lives of others, especially your child.

My goal is to make you more aware of the power invested in you so that when you speak, Heaven responds and demons tremble. Nations are feared by other nations because of the rumors of the many battles they have won. Just imagine defeating the enemy time and time again that your name and your child's name are being whispered in hell as forces that cannot be reckoned with. I'm expecting sweatless victories with the devil and his cohorts, and so should you. Before we move on, I would like to provide some basic information about this kingdom of darkness we wrestle against and its hierarchy. Shall class begin?

War in the Heavenlies

In order to understand how we got here, let's go back to the beginning. Long, long ago, before Jesus came to earth, before Moses, and even before Adam and Eve. There is a story that if understood helps explain the present war in the heavenlies. The story of the fall of lucifer is outlined over multiple Scriptures, but Ezekiel 28 is a good place to start.

Reader beware—disappointing biography ahead:

Son of man, sing this funeral song for the king of Tyre. Give him this message from the Sovereign Lord: "You were the model of perfection, full of wisdom and exquisite in beauty. You were in Eden, the garden of God. Your clothing was adorned with every precious stone—red carnelian, pale-green peridot, white moonstone, blue-green beryl, onyx, green jasper, blue lapis lazuli, turquoise, and emerald—all beautifully crafted for you and set in the finest gold. They were given to you on the day you were created. I ordained and anointed you as the mighty angelic guardian. You had access to the holy mountain of God and walked among the stones of fire. You were blameless in all you did from the day you were created until the day evil was found in you. Your rich commerce led you to violence, and you sinned. So I banished you in disgrace from the mountain of God. I expelled you, O mighty guardian, from your place among the stones of fire. Your heart was filled with pride because of all your beauty. Your wisdom was corrupted by your love of splendor. So I threw you to the ground and exposed you to the curious gaze of kings. You defiled your sanctuaries with your many sins and your dishonest trade. So I brought fire out from within you, and it consumed you. I reduced you to ashes on the ground in the sight of all who were watching" (Ezekiel 28:12-18 NLT).

More Scripture to build a complete picture:

And another sign appeared in heaven: behold, a great dragon, with seven heads and ten horns, and on his heads seven diadems. His tail swept down a third of the stars of heaven and cast them to the earth (Revelation 12:3-4).

Satan Thrown Down to Earth

Then there was war in heaven. Michael and his angels fought against the dragon and his angels. And the dragon lost the battle, and he and his angels were forced out of heaven. This great dragon—the ancient serpent called the devil, or Satan, the one deceiving the whole world—was thrown down to the earth with all his angels (Revelation 12:7-9 NLT).

When lucifer fell and took with him one-third of the angels as described in the Book of Revelation, he fell from a glorious position where truth and light reigned to a place where he now must blind and deceive just to get followers. What a pathetic existence. In the time it took for God to separate darkness from His presence, his name went from lucifer, son of the morning star, to satan: the enemy of God, the lord of evil, father of lies, the god of this age, the devil, beelzebub.

Satan's followers, the fallen third, went from angels, meaning messengers, to demons, evil spirits, devils, unclean spirits, fallen angels, false messenger, principalities, powers, rulers, wickedness in high places, liars, familiar spirits, and enemies of all that is true and represent truth.

You must understand that their agenda is to get as many of us to go to hell with them as possible, to stop us from reaching and achieving our God-given purpose while here on earth, and to curse the loving hands that hold us together.

Like in all kingdoms, whether the kingdom of darkness or Kingdom of light, there are levels of authority and hierarchies. The Bible provides some insight into the hierarchy of the kingdom of darkness, so let's look at what it has to say about the lowest level, "familiar spirits."

Why Is a Spirit Familiar?

The root of familiar and spirit come from *yada,* a Hebrew word that means: to know, a knowing one; specifically, a conjurer.

With this understanding, familiar spirits are used to deceive and report on the life of someone who may have passed on; we cannot ignore the element that in order to do that, they must have assignments of knowing and spying to accurately provide an update or report. Let's consider the following article by Matt Slick, president and founder of the Christian Apologetics and Research Ministry. I believe he does a great job articulating the fundamentals of what these spirits are:

> "A familiar spirit is a demon that is summoned by a medium with the intention that the spirit summoned will obey his or her commands. Often, familiar spirits are believed to be the spirits of people who have died

(Deut. 18:11). However, many commentators argue that biblically this is not the case. Such appearances are in actuality demonic forces imitating people in order to deceive."

"The two words 'familiar spirit' are translated into the English language from the single Hebrew word obe."[1]

Familiar Spirits are Great Note Takers

Theologians also argue that these spirits are assigned to us from conception and even potentially from birth, they create reports of actions and responses, likes, and dislikes, their full-time job is you and your child. They are messengers of evil, they communicate to each other and to higher ruling spirits of darkness. Familiar spirits are used many times in dealings with fortune tellers or by those who claim to be able to speak to the dead. The familiar spirit of the fortune teller is speaking to the familiar spirit of the dead person, therefore relaying messages to the ear of the teller, because these spirits are evil in nature they tell lies, and incomplete truths, so many times people are getting their lives guided by a lying spirit, that is why the Word of God admonishes us to not pay any attention to familiar spirits or mediums: *"Do not turn to mediums or spiritists; do not seek them out to be defiled by them I am the Lord your God"* (Leviticus 19:31).

I can never forget the disturbing news I received concerning who were frequent patrons of a particular psychic: Christians, pastors, and leaders in the church. This group was seeking direction, answers, and strategies because they themselves could not hear from God. It reminds me of the Bible story when King Saul sought a medium because *"God has left me"* (1 Samuel 28:3-25 NLT).

Do you now see why it's so important to teach your children to war and how to hear the loving voice of God for themselves? We are admonished *not* to consult soothsayers, fortune tellers, psychics, etc. because satan and his cohort's job is to steal, kill, and destroy. It would be their pleasure and a demonic joke to direct you into a job, marriage, or situation that would end up being the most dreadful experience of your life.

Let's Go Diving

To better understand our opponents in this battle, let's take a deep dive into the next group of fallen angels: principalities, powers, and rulers.

Ephesians 6:12 (KJV) says, *"For we wrestle not against flesh and blood, but against principalities, against powers, against the rulers of the darkness of this world, against spiritual wickedness in high places."*

Author remix: my version of Ephesians 6:12 is, "For we are not in a fight with mere human flesh, men, women, skin, or bones, but against a renegade of disobedient angels who lost their crown of glory by getting evicted from the presence of God and desperately desire and want you to get evicted too."

Ephesians 6:12 says that we are fighting against principalities that are magistracy, leaders, and those in great authority over regions. We are also fighting powers, which are dark forces that try to influence your choices, physical, mental power, and abilities. We are fighting rulers of the darkness of this world, which are leaders whose commands and demands are heard and responded to by evil spirit perpetrators. As you can see, we have multiple enemies.

The enemy that you can see, the bully at your child's school, or the nasty mean girl on the playground is just a mere host being used to carry out the plans of the unseen dark commanders in charge. Ephesians 6:12 is so very helpful in providing us types of demonic forces that rage against us and our children. Let's look at each one in more detail to broaden our understanding and to teach to our children.

We Are Fighting Against Principalities

Principalities are magistracy, leaders, and those in great authority over regions. Perry Stone, who I absolutely admire, pens in his book, *Feeding Demons,* what a principality really is. Let's look at his summaries with the hope of gaining a deeper level of understanding.

> "Among the top four demonic agents, the principality holds the highest rank. The Greek word for 'principalities' is arche, meaning 'first ones' or 'leaders.' These spirits wield the highest level of authority and are directly under satan's command."

> "Principalities are the unseen spirits that dominate visible world governments, through controlling the minds of leaders to pass laws (such as laws against praying in public (Dan. 6) or designating laws to prevent the Gospel message from reaching the nation."

> "There are entire nations closed to the preaching of

the Gospel: China, North Vietnam, the Arabian Gulf States and so forth."[2]

We Are Fighting Against Powers

"The next level of agents are 'powers,' the Greek word here being exousia, translated as 'authorities.' While opinions differ, these are the spirits working in more localized regions and were the types of spirits Christ encountered throughout His ministry. These would include 'foul spirits' and 'unclean spirits' (Mark 9:35; Matt. 10:1). The words foul and unclean are the same Greek word, akatharlos, indicating they are morally unclean and inspire lewd and immoral actions."[3]

We Are Fighting Against Rulers

"The 'rulers of darkness of this world' are spirits that prey on not just physical darkness but the mental darkness in the minds of humanity. Darkness is the absence of light, and when the Gospel is preached darkness is expelled. These rulers of darkness are the spirits in nations that attempt to maintain strongholds on individuals who exercise some type of authority, to hinder in any manner the presentation of the Gospel."[4]

While studying these arch spirits, I have learned that their tactics have never really changed over centuries of time. They love using intimidation and the spirit of fear to keep us frozen and in a defensive position. The deception is, if we don't fight back, they will just leave us alone. But the truth of the matter is, the enemy doesn't want to simply run us over one time. *If* he had the opportunity, he would back the car up and repeat the process over and over again, leaving us a bloody, dismantled mess, a sign to others saying, "Don't mess with me." Notice the word, *If he had the opportunity....* You must know as a child of the Most High God that would never happen. It's contradictory to God's Word because that would be unbearable!

Even in the attacks there are limitations to how far they can go. Some attacks are sovereignly explained and sovereignly allowed, our example for this is in the Book of Job. Others are caused because we have not locked the doors we should have bolted shut. Therefore, we created self-inflicted unnecessary wounds due to our ignorance or even disobedience. Either way, it's important for us as parents to first be empowered in order to empower our children how to shut the doors and keep them closed tightly.

OK Fear, You're Next

There are many kinds of spirits, but the one I *really* want to expose is the spirit of fear. That particular spirit has literally plagued me for more than half of my life; so, I have a personal vendetta against it.

Fear is defined in many ways, but one of my favorite acronyms is: "False Evidence Appearing Real." Most of the time what we are fearing is an exaggerated version of an idea that was planted in our minds by an influencing spirit, possibly through conversations, radio, television, that has now been blown out of proportion.

I used to have a bad fear of speaking in front of people. I would torture myself with ideas of people getting up and walking out, or people beginning to laugh out loud at me while I spoke, and so on. For years, those particular images in my mind kept me from doing many things I know I was called to do such as teach, sing, dance, and write books, all of which are reasons why I was created. Once I allowed God to do open heart surgery on me and by faith doing what God was requiring of me, I realized that all my fear-driven images were lying, imposter thoughts.

The one thing I do know about fear is that it is a transferable spirit and is extremely contagious. This spirit can be easily spread and downloaded to our children. To this day I am still working with my children on fears that I believe transferred to them by either myself or my husband. My reality is that fear was not broken off my life until after I had my kids; so in a few instances they are fighting what I did not conquer before they were born.

When I was pregnant and carrying my firstborn son, fear at that time simply put, ruled my life. I was a single mother taking on a brand-new responsibility and that terrified me. I feared being alone. I feared being a bad mother, not being able to take care of my child. I was scared my child was going to have some kind of disorder. I feared him being ugly, sorry just keeping it real. All those fears plus more bottled up in my mind and soul controlled me, ultimately allowing my son to be tormented by the same spirit while in my womb. While pregnant, I not only was carrying fear but my son as well, therefore fear felt empowered to become a fraternal twin to my son. But it wasn't counting on me catching a revelation as fast as I did. It never got the chance to take over his life as it did mine, so hallelujah for that!

The sooner you catch these spiritual principles, the greater ground your children will cover at an earlier age. I believe that there was a deliberate plan and contract out on my son when he was yet in my womb, as most children are targeted by the evil one. I prophesy that our seeds will, like Christ, crush the head of every serpent.

The Enemy Wants to Scare Us to Death

The enemy has an all-out assault against the seed and the seed carrier. I remember being pregnant and not being able to sleep for three of the ten months of pregnancy—yes, ten months, a full-term pregnancy is 40 weeks—due to being attacked at night. For three months straight, as long as it was dark outside, I could not get any peace. There were many times when I would fall asleep from being exhausted and simply pregnant. But I would soon feel a tapping until I woke up. Yet I was in the room completely by myself.

Another tactic from the enemy was when I would fall asleep, I would hear someone calling my name. When I awakened I was, again, by myself. Experiencing this for the first time in my life and at the most vulnerable time in my life was frightening and devastating. Going to many spiritual "authorities" in the faith and never getting the answers that would lead to peace only strengthened my belief that I was weak, and the devil was stronger. There were moments when the tormenting would cease, but then it returned with a vengeance a few days later. This spirit called fear was having a field day with me during a time when I should have been enjoying the maturation of my unborn child.

The Enemy Does Not Fight Fair

I continued to suffer through it until the attacks moved from me to my son after he was born. During the delivery of my son, he almost died as a result of the umbilical cord being wrapped around his neck and the doctors didn't know it. For many of the nineteen hours of labor, he was receiving limited amounts of oxygen. I know the plan of the enemy was to abort my seed that day; but when God has a plan for your life, you must know that He will use all of Heaven's resources to ensure its manifestation into the earth realm.

The enemy does not fight fair, and if he can abort Heaven's plans early on, the less work he has to do when the boy becomes a man.

The Score: Fear 95 – Parent 120

How do you assist in breaking fear in your child? I'm glad you asked. One of the first important ways is to always ask the Holy Spirit to reveal the root of entry. If it's in the womb, renounce or break covenant with any open doors that you as the parent may have had during that time. If it's a traumatic situation, minister healing, love, and comfort. One major point of advice I want to deliver—do not allow your children to miss opportunities simply because they are afraid. My children will tell you what my response would be if they say to me, "I want to do it, but I'm really afraid." My rebuttal always is, "Do it afraid until you're afraid no more." I never allow fear to be the reason for missing an activity or opportunity.

Story Time

My second child was around six or seven years old at the time we had the following conversation in the car going to her first track meet. Let me provide you a quick backdrop. Kristian was the kind of child who even when she was very young, she was a naturally fast runner. I remember when she was in her walker before she could walk on her own and she would literally speed race from one end of the house to the other, while laughing hysterically. We saw very early on that she was born to run.

Fast forward to our conversation in the car. On our way to her first track meet of the season, she just kept crying saying, "I can't do it, I can't do it. I'm too afraid." I knew at that moment the sneaky spirit of fear that kept me from running, playing basketball, and so many other things was trying to be bold enough to rob my child. I became righteously indignant; I do that a lot.

I looked in her tear-filled eyes and said, "I rebuke that spirit of fear. Kristian, God has NOT given you the spirit of fear but of POWER! You're going to use the power of God to get down that track. I love you; but if I must get out there on that track with you, *you WILL run today."*

Whether it was the prayer or the thought of her mom running with her, she stopped crying, powered up, and ran. A first-place medal was her reward for not allowing fear to win that day. Fast forward seven years later from that day, Kristian is now a nationally ranked runner and running high school level times—and she's only in the eighth grade. Her dream is to one day run in the Olympics; and I believe as she continues to daily decline fear's invitation to dance in her life, she absolutely will make her dream come true!

The Enemy Never Uses His PTO (Planned Time Off)

The enemy's job is to challenge God in His plans and purposes for humankind and that includes you and your child. He thought he won when he deceived Eve in the Garden of Eden, when he crucified Jesus, and when he attacks you as a believer. But what the enemy intends for evil, God will turn around for your good, plans, and purposes.

Our heavenly Father is the master spiritual chess player, the greatest of all time. I have learned that most highly ranked chess players can predict their opponents moves seven to eleven-plus moves ahead. Well, our heavenly Father can anticipate and put a plan into place for moves eternally long. Now take that, satan!

UNDERSTANDING CHANGES EVERYTHING.

Understand this concept: just because satan can quote Scriptures, doesn't mean he knows it. He failed the class of spiritual comprehension because he lacks the revealer of all truths, the Holy Spirit. The Word of God is Spirit-breathed and

Spirit-discerned. You need to fully understand these fundamental truths to be able to download them into your children in practical ways. Do not fret, the purpose of this book is to help provide those tips. *Remember, you must first understand in order to help your child understand.* Once you get it, understanding can change everything.

Proverbs 4:7 (KJV) says, *"With all thy getting get understanding."*

Selah Moment—aka Pause and Think

Points to Ponder

- You are in a fixed fight where you have already won.
- Greater is HE who is in you, then he who is in the world.
- The enemy is a great illusionist, don't believe the hype.
- Fear: A bad thought that has awakened your emotions to believe it's real.
- The enemy is a master illusionist, do not fall for his false illusions.

Prayer Time:

Father, I thank You for revealing through Your Word the devices of our enemies. Now, Father, I ask for the spirit of wisdom and revelation to come into my life. Reveal the unhealthy roots in my life and in the lives of my children so that You can destroy those roots and heal us. I choose to decline all of fear's invitations and will walk in power, love, and a sound mind. I declare that greater are You in me than he that is in the world.

Prayer Declaration

Lord, I declare that _____
(insert your child's name) *is more than a conquer, and as You teach our hands to war through reading this book, we are hidden under the shadow of Your wings, hidden and protected by Your love and grace. I declare that no weapon formed against us will be prosper, and my child will learn how to condemn every word that rises up against him/her in judgment. In Jesus's name, amen.*

Summary Activation:
Let's Change the Channel

Ask your child to close his or her eyes. Now say, "Picture yourself eating your favorite ice cream cone or favorite treat." Many times, you will get a giggle out of the child when you do this. Once the scene of eating is confirmed, say, "Now, open your eyes."

Have a conversation explaining that the same place they saw themselves eating their ice cream cone, is the same movie screen that the enemy wants to take over, pollute, and provide thoughts and images that are simply "not good." The enemy will try to place fears there, but they have the power to erase them, make them disappear.

We must train our kids to change the channel of the movie in their mind. You can do this activity every day to get them well trained on learning how to change the way they think. This is a skill adults need to learn as well, because as we think in our heart, so we are.

Breaking Any Lies Prayer

Father, expose any false perceptions and lies that I am believing about You. Dismantle the filters that say You are not for me and that You're not a good Father. I break agreement with any ideas or thoughts that say You want to harm me and You like to see me suffer. Amen.

Breaking Fear Prayer

Father, I break covenant with the spirit of fear. Fear no longer has any authority to rule or reign in my life. I will do the will of God. I will move forward with dreams and pursue God opportunities. I exchange any filters of fears with the eyes of Christ. I will see my life through God's eyes. Father, as I write down my fears and the fears of my child, I am giving them over to You, and I give You full permission to uproot them out of our lives once and for all.

List your fears and the fears of your child, then pray over each fear, that it would be replaced with the peace and will of God.

Parent Child

_____

_____

_____

_____

_____

_____

_____

_____

_____

_____

_____

_____

ENDNOTES

1. Matt Slick, "What is a familiar spirit?"; https://carm.org/what-is-a
    -familiar-spirit; accessed December 20, 2019.
2. Perry Stone Jr., _Feeding Demons_ (Austin, TX: The Fedd Agency,
    Inc., 2017).
3. Ibid.
4. Ibid.

Chapter Three

CURIOSITY CAN OPEN DOORS

"I Think It's Charlie"

It was no later than 2:00 A.M. when I was awakened by the terrifying screams of my nine-year-old daughter violently banging on our bedroom door. As a parent, I can tell what screams are really filled with fear and terror, and this one most definitely qualified in that category. Immediately I jumped from the bed to grab the doorknob, which felt like minutes instead of the actual seconds it took me to swing open our bedroom door as fast as I could.

Kristian wrapped her arms around me, hysterically crying. All I saw was fear, tears, and terror all over her. I shouted over her belting, "What's wrong, Kristian. What's wrong?" All she kept saying was, "Something's in my room, something's in my room and it moved my shoes and medals."

My first thought was an animal or something was in her room, but I remembered her medals were hanging on the wall, so that idea was quickly thrown out of the window. It took about fifteen minutes to calm her down long enough to get an understanding of what was really happening.

As I sat her on my bed, I slowing asked her to tell me what she saw and experienced. Her first clear statement was, "I think its Charlie and he's in my room!" Huh? At that moment I was presented with two options, pass out or *power up!*

"Who the Heck Is Charlie?"

Let me digress and fill you in on Mr. Charlie Charlie. For many years in Mexico there was a game young children played at recess and in school yards titled Charlie, Charlie. Wikipedia describes the game as follows: "The Charlie Charlie challenge is a modern incarnation of a Spanish paper-and-pencil game called Juego de la Lapicera (Pencil Game). Like a Magic 8-Ball, the game is played by teenagers using held or balanced pencils to produce answers to questions they ask. Teenage girls have played Juego de la Lapicera for generations in Spain and Hispanic America, asking which boys in their class like them."

This game's origin and premise was amplified when coming into the US in 2015. At some point, the game escalated into the idea of "conjuring up the spirit of a young boy, named Charlie, who violently died in a car accident." Based on its basic fundamental rules and similar strategies of play, the game is being coined the poor man's Ouija board. Like the Ouija board, this game has rules, and if the child, breaks certain rules, such as not asking Charlie's permission to exit the game, according to the escalated US version of the game, the spirit of Charlie will follow you home to "taunt or torment" you.

Let me add some more context and backdrop to this story. Approximately three weeks before the banging on the door screaming episode, our family was having a family discussion at dinner. My son, who at the time was in middle school, brought up a situation that really disturbed him that day in school. He started the story off by saying, "Mom and Dad, you may get an email from my principal today." Immediately my parental walls began to rise, but I put my game face on long enough to hear "his side" of the story. He told us how he got into a verbal altercation with some kids in the lunchroom because they were going to make and play a game called, Charlie Charlie.

I asked my son, "Who is Charlie?" Kamryn, who was eleven years old, began to share the history of Charlie, how to play the game, and what it was all about. After he was finished, I promise you, my jaw was in my mashed potatoes. I wanted to ask him, "What ever happened to playing jacks or Double Dutch at school?" but I didn't.

Kamryn continued to tell the story of the lunchroom incident. Not only did he tell the kids that they shouldn't be playing the game, he also told one of the girls who was offended at his assertion, that he rebuked her in Jesus's name and all her evil spirits. After that statement, he ran and told a teacher what was happening at the school lunchroom table, because apparently playing this game was prohibited.

After Kamryn's, "I rebuke you in Jesus's name" statement, this young lady started crying and the school was going to email us, notifying us that Kamryn was "calling names" (insert face palm emoji right here, lol).

I asked Kamryn, "Did you really say, 'I rebuke you'?" He chuckled a little and said, "I sure did." My next thought was, *Where were all the teachers while all of this was happening?* Anyway, we continued to eat our dinner while my secret thought was, *Good job, Kam, so proud of you. We have our very own demon buster in the house.*

I know what you're thinking, *Is she ever going to get back to the episode with her daughter?* Don't worry, stay with me, I am.

Kamryn concluded the story with how disgusted he was that those kids would even attempt such a thing, he continued to rant about consequences and what it really means to play with satanic games and why you should not try to communicate with "the dark side." As an opportunity to get more understanding, we invited Kristian in on the conversation, asked her for her opinion and inquired if any kids were playing the game at her school? She very nonchalantly said, "Hmm, no, I don't think so."

OK, now let's go back to the story.

After hearing Kristian, my nine-year-old, state that Charlie was in her room, I was presented with two options, either pass out or *power up*—and power up was exactly what I did. As soon as she said the name Charlie. I quickly remembered the conversation at the dinner table and all of the education I received on this topic. Recounting this information caused my adrenaline to soar through the roof and my spiritual blood to boil. My first thought was, *Charlie picked the wrong child to follow home!* And my second one was, *I'm sending Charlie back to hell.*

I grabbed my little Charlie door opener by the arm, stood up and said, "Not in my house, I have authority here. Come on, we are sending Charlie back to where he came from." She cried and even screamed a little. I remember my husband looking at us both like we had three heads. He knew I wasn't joking and understood that this lesson must be played out. I looked her directly in the face and said "Kris, the enemy and Charlie are trespassing in my house. They cannot harm you, and that's why it only tried to scare you by moving your medals and shoes. You opened up this door, now we must close it. God is with us, I am with you, and I will help you. I will not allow fear to take over and win."

I literally pulled her up the stairs, pushed open the door of her bedroom and shouted "Charlie! This is MY house and you are trespassing. Kristian lives under my roof and we all are under the authority of Jesus Christ." I'm not going to lie; my spirit was in fact sensing something dark and evil in that room that night, but I refused to allow what I was sensing to bully me or my child. I coached her on renouncing and closing all doors opened by curiosity. I continued to coach her on telling Charlie to leave in the name of Jesus and then I took over. I declared the Word of God over that room and our home. I shouted what was written until we both felt Heaven and earth collide.

I prayed a prayer similar to this:

"Father, in the name of Jesus, I thank You that You have given us the authority to trample on the head of serpents, scorpions, and Charlie. Because all authority has been given to us, we bind up any evil spirits and take back any authority that may have been given over because of curiosity or disobedience.

"Father, we thank You that Your presence is here, that Your presence is the ruling presence in this room and in this home. We thank You that whatever is bound in this room is being bound in heavenly places, and whatever is loosed in this room is being loosed in heavenly places. Dear God, we loose Your peace, we loose Your rest, and we loose Your glory in Kristian's room. We thank You, Father, that You hover over Kristian, that she is Yours, and if anything tries to harm her it will have to go through You. In Jesus's name we pray, amen."

After about fifteen minutes of praying, declaring, renouncing, and cleaning up her room, she too felt the peace that simply surpassed our understanding.

> ...*The Lord is at hand; do not be anxious about anything, but in everything by prayer and supplication with thanksgiving let your requests be made known to God. And the peace of God, which surpasses all understanding, will guard your hearts and your minds in Christ Jesus* (Philippians 4:5-7 English Standard Version).

I hugged her, loved on her, and affirmed her. She lay back down on her bed, *in her room*, and fell asleep. Charlie nor anything else ever returned.

Before I move on, I want to address a few questions you may be asking yourself after reading this story. You may be wondering:

Question: *Why would she make her child go back into a place of fear? Or, why would she make her go back upstairs when she was so afraid, couldn't that traumatize a young child?*

Answer: These are great questions, and I'm glad you asked. The one thing that I have learned over the years is that if you do not conquer fear, it will conquer you. Fear typically travels with its cousins—torment, unrest, and anxiety. I heard the Holy Spirit specifically say to me that night, "She must resist and overcome this fear." If I pacified her and allowed her to sleep in my room or become bullied by this spirit, I knew that it would be harder the next day or week to uproot and eventually conquer.

Fear has a very skillful way of magnifying its illusions to appear real, bigger, and stronger than us or the God we serve. Also, if this spirit is allowed to remain, there will be an open door that empowers the enemy to infiltrate in other ways. When we fear, we are idolizing the thing we are afraid of, especially if it stops us from being obedient to God's will for our lives. Ultimately, if we fear, we are saying something else is bigger than God, and that's why I put it in the idol category.

Let me say it like this. The very thing you fear rules you, controls you, and will have its own way with you. Deuteronomy 31:8 (NIV) says, *"The Lord himself goes before you and will be with you; he will never leave you nor forsake you. Do not be afraid; do not be discouraged."*

Fear is the opposite thought of God's. We are instructed not to fear because what we fear becomes an idol in our lives. When we fear, we are saying it's too big for my Father to handle. If we disobey God and listen to fear, we have exalted it above Him. As we discussed in Chapter One, any thought opposite of God's is thinking from another kingdom, the dark one. There are two ruling kingdoms constantly vying for operation in our lives—what kingdom are they living out of when we allow our children to remain in fear and use it as a filter to live through? The dark one. Rather, we must destroy all idols and fear to allow God's Kingdom to reign.

Having a foundational understanding of the cause of Kristian's torment, I also knew that because she was the one who opened the door, and because she was old enough, it would be more effective if she was the one to close it. We will discuss closing doors more in Chapter Eight. Since I am always looking for opportunities to train her in the ways of God, I felt like this was a great lesson in the importance of telling the truth, being aware of what doors are being opened by curiosity, and closing doors 101.

Question: *What was the open door of access to allow an evil spirit to invade your home?*

Answer: Great question. The next day I was able to chat with Kristian more about what happened. She told me that she was not honest when we asked her three weeks prior if the Charlie Charlie game was being played in her school. She wasn't honest because a few of her friends did actually play the game, and even though she did not physically partake in the activity, she did confess that she watched because she was *curious* to see if the pencils were going to spin and move on their own.

She also confirmed that the pencils did in fact spin when they asked Charlie a question which shows there was some kind of *allowable* infiltration. Once that happened, she said while she was watching, one of the little boys who built the game, turned and looked at her to scare her and said, "Now Charlie Charlie is coming to *your* house." Fear set into her heart and she felt responsible if anything were to happen; so instead of coming clean, it was just easier at the time to deny and hope for the best. Lying is not only an open door to the enemy but fear begets more fears. It must be uprooted from its core; if allowed to remain, it will take over your life.

At the time, what my daughter did not understand was that her curiosity was the vehicle used to allow her to be open and engaged with whatever was happening almost to the same extent as if she was playing it herself. All the enemy needs is a crack of an opening, agreement, or openness from curiosity to infiltrate and disturb. The pencils moving, something completely out of her wheelhouse, opened her up to the spirit of fear, and fear opened the door for whatever else to creep on in and infiltrate.

Question: *How did you know what to say or pray?*

Answer: Prior experiences prepared me for how to handle this particular situation. Out of those prior experiences the one thing that stuck with me was how God is with us and will never leave us. If God be for us, who can be against us—and that goes for anything living in the kingdom of darkness, including Charlie.

> *But the Advocate, the Holy Spirit, whom the Father will send in my name, will teach you all things and will remind you of everything I have said to you* (John 14:26 NIV).

It's very important to develop the spiritual skill of hearing and being led by the Holy Spirit (discussed in Chapter Six). He is the Comforter and Teacher of all things. He will bring all things back to your remembrance. When we don't know what to say or pray, the Holy Spirit does, so just ask Him.

Last, I also know what God's Word says about the authority we have and how to use that authority to dismantle the plans of the enemy. The enemy had a plan to spiritually bully and terrorize my daughter that night, what he didn't account for was a mother who knew who she was. Reading the Bible and knowing your place in God's Kingdom is crucial.

Question: *Were you afraid?*

Answer: At first, yes! The screams alone sent my emotions on a roller coaster ride. *But,* I have learned that the enemy feeds off our fear, so I very quickly broke agreement with fear. I kept thinking to myself, *God, You have not given me the spirit of fear but of love, power, and a sound mind* (2 Timothy 1:7 NKJV).

I knew I could not give in to what I was feeling. I could not afford to accept fear's invitation to dance; so this time, I simply declined. This sounds easy now, but if you remember reading Chapter One, it wasn't always that cut and dry for me, nor was I always able to quickly go through these steps and simply decline. There was a process and journey that I had to go through that encouraged my faith in what God's Word says about me and the authority I carry.

Knowledge is a weapon as stated in Hosea 4:6 (English Standard Version) in the Word: *"My people are destroyed for lack of knowledge; because you have rejected knowledge, I reject you from being a priest to me. And since you have forgotten the law of your God, I also will forget your children."*

Simply not knowing does not automatically give you or your child a pass from being attacked or infiltrated by the enemy and his dark forces. Witchcraft is now being sold to our children in pretty pink packages. From elementary school on up, classrooms are riddled with terminology that attempts to indoctrinate our children to believe that the fundamentals of witchcraft are OK. Math wizard, word spells, good witch, fairy godmothers, good goblins, and white ghost are just some of the terms that our children from kindergarten are becoming accustomed to hearing. Those all were real title headers on class work I have seen over the years with my own kids. What do spells have to do with English or math? My answer would be, "nothing." I believe these actions are attempts to sow visual indoctrinations and opportunities to desensitize our children to what the Word says is evil.

While in the process of writing this particular book, something happened in my home and I just knew I had to add it to the book and share with you. My husband found a pretty pink journal in my stepdaughter's room titled *School of Awake,* endorsed by Oprah Winfrey. At the first glance, looking at this hot pink cover of the book, we clearly understood why it was so inviting to engage with, especially to a middle school age girl. But being knowledgeable about symbolisms and knowing that Oprah's endorsements not always crown Jesus King, we took it from underneath her pillow and our investigation began. Many terms immediately leaped out to us. The first was Heartstar. Per this book:

> "The Heartstar will never steer you wrong or leave you. Your Heartstar has been with you since you were born and loves you more than anyone in the world. It is always available, whenever you need counsel. Consider your Heartstar your built in GPS that wants to guide you to be the best version of yourself. It's your bestie. When you get quiet and breathe, our Heartstar is waiting to give us the answer we need."

After more research regarding this book I found at charaka .com that:

> "The symbol for the heart chakra is composed of the following elements: A six-pointed star or hexagram,

also referred to as shaktona; Twelve petals positioned in circle, depicted with the a rich color red or vermilion; this part of the symbol is sometimes referred to as a twelve-petaled lotus flower; In the Hindu tradition, the deity associated with the heart chakra is Vayu, who sits at the center of the symbol, riding an antelope or deer; Inside the main circle, we can find another eight-petaled circle, also referred to as eight-petaled lotus (in the Hindu tradition)."

The Enemy Loves to Steal

Here's the deal with this, the enemy is nothing but a thief and a robber. He does not have one creative bone in his miserable body. When reading the paragraph on the heartstar in the book, we quickly understood and it became very clear that this book was anchored in the New Age religion. They say, "heartstar," we say Holy Spirit. The world is so good at stealing biblical truths, changing the wording, repackaging it, and redirecting glory to an unknown source, a demonic one. I implore you as a parent to open your eyes and keep them open. Every person, song, or book selling peace, love, and harmony is not anchored or sourced by the Kingdom of God.

If we as parents are not aware of these devices being used to divert our children's affections, our kids will be polluted with doctrines that war up against the true knowledge of who God really is. They will also unknowingly open themselves up to other voices that would love to detour their destinies and minimize their authority and call. We must educate them on all of the wolves in sheep's clothing.

As Hosea 4:6 instructs us to seek Heaven's knowledge, we are not simply left alone by the enemy because we are ignorant of the impacts we have allowed. When indulging in other religions or things God calls detestable—divination, idols, witchcraft, sorcery, casting spells, mediums, spirits, calling upon the dead, poltergeists, magic—we also open ourselves up to judgment and the consequences of indulging.

Deuteronomy 18:9-13 in The Message Bible says:

> *When you enter the land that God, your God, is giving you, don't take on the abominable ways of life of the nations there. Don't you dare sacrifice your son or daughter in the fire.* **Don't practice divination, sorcery, fortune telling, witchery, casting spells, holding séances, or channeling with the dead. People who do these things are an abomination to God.** *It's because of just such abominable practices that God, your God, is driving these nations out before you.* **Be completely loyal to God, your God.**

How to cast spells and operate in powers fueled by hell is being marketed to our children daily through music, television, books, classrooms, and movies. These concepts are speaking to and feeding an already natural desire to be powerful, rule, reign, and have dominion. When uncovering some very alarming hidden messages in today's music and movies being used to infiltrate the hearts of our young ones, remember that God is still in control. Parents are God's first line of defense—be aware of the devil's tactics.

Are there an "Trojan Horses" in your home?

In 2004, a film was released titled, *Troy* that was loosely based on Homer's Iliad. The film was one of my favorites to watch because it encompassed heroism, battles of war, suspense, romance, and so many other things. I remember watching the movie that starred Brad Pitt who masterfully played the part of the arch and formidable enemy of Troy. As a result of a triangle affair that involved a princess, a prince and a King, Greece decided to wage war against Troy. There was a point in the movie when the opposing enemy, Greece, realized that the walls of their enemy (Troy) were impenetrable. A scheme was concocted to portray the appearance of a retreat and leave a gift for Troy as a "peace offering." The Grecian army left a huge "Trojan Horse" on the beach hoping the City of Troy would take it inside their walls. I hope this is not a spoiler moment for those who have not seen the movie, but I am sad to say that they actually did accept that beautiful gift into their gates. Late in the middle of the night, the Grecian soldiers who were hiding in the Trojan horse, crept out, opened the gates to their army who was hiding in a cove, came in and completely devoured the city.

Like the city of Troy, we too are a Kingdom and the enemy desires to present alluring gifts that are really purposed to undo us from within. I hear parents say quite often, "*it's not that bad.*" I can hear the shaky compromise in their voices and question, "why is any amount of uncertainty a good enough guarantee of security for our children?" Why isn't the standard, 100% surety?

Do Not Fear

I want to present some questions that will provoke some soul searching for you and your child:

- Are you aware of the games being played at recess or books that are being given to your child to read that have subliminal demonic roots?
- Do you know if your child has been exposed to any occult-rooted activities?
- Do you really know if your child's online browsing practices are healthy?

If you don't know, please do not feel condemned. Many parents do not know what signs to look for or the questions to ask to uncover possible infiltrations into their child's life. That is why I decided to write this book. If you don't know, it's time for you to get some answers.

Points to Ponder

- Remind your child about the importance of telling the truth.
- You have authority to dismantle the plans of the enemy.
- Curiosity can be a door opener.
- Any open door can be closed; do not fear.
- The Holy Spirit is real and He desires to teach and comfort you and your child.

- Knowledge is a weapon; the enemy does not care if we remain ignorant.
- Teach your child to break covenant and renounce any connections they have with the kingdom of darkness.

It's Investigation Time

Throughout this chapter there were several probing questions asked of you to answer. If you do not have the answers to those questions or the following ones, pause before moving forward and have the necessary conversations with your child to gain better insight. If it takes a week, it takes a week. Try not to make your child feel interrogated; present the questions as part of a conversation.

Hi _____ *(insert child's name)*, let's chat.

The following are suggested questions to ask your child:

1. What are your thoughts about magic?
2. On a scale of 1-5, how fearful are you? How often do you feel afraid?
3. On a scale of 1-5, how much do you like yourself?
4. How much do you love Jesus? From zero to five and five being a whole bunch.
5. Do any of the kids in your school talk about spells or being a wizard?
6. If a friend invited you to play a game that talks to ghosts or spirits, what would you do?

Chapter Four

THE ENEMY IS AT THE GATE

Who's Guarding the Gate?

Whoever controls the gate of a city controls the city. The gate of a city is the entry point to where goods and services enter in and out. Where food, resources, and life sustaining elements enter in. Much like a city, we too have gates. The goal of the enemy is to enter the gates of our children with the supreme goal of spoiling what's inside.

When I speak of gates, I am specifically speaking to entry points that allow something to influence the way a child thinks, perceives, dreams, and lives. Your natural eyes are gates, your natural ears are gates, and other gates are touch and even smell. In this chapter we will cover the first two: eyes and ears. While digging deeper into hearing and sight, we will look at guarding these gates from the perspective of prevention, by keeping doors shut off to the enemy who *crouches at the door and waits for any opportunity* to jump in and devour us (see Genesis 4:7; 1 Peter 5:8).

Much of how we think and react is connected directly to what we are consistently exposed to. What we hear, see, touch, and feel is intricately connected to our life filters. We are the sum total of the thoughts that are sourced by these senses. What we hear over and over will eventually formulate a life doctrine, or faith, for how we respond and live.

Deliverance is great, and Christ died so that we can be set free from the influence of demonic infestations; but Jesus also lived a life that we ourselves should want to model to prevent a demonic infiltration. There is a need for parents to be aware of the necessity to guard their children's gates as well as teach them how to guard their own. As parents, it is so important to be aware of what your children are seeing and hearing. What really is standing in their gates?

Please Turn on the Lights

Luke 11:34-36 (NKJV) says:

> *The lamp of the body is the eye. Therefore, when your eye is good, your whole body also is full of light. But when your eye is bad, your body also is full of darkness. Therefore take heed that the light which is in you is not darkness. If then your whole body is full of light, having no part dark, the whole body will be full of light, as when the bright shining of a lamp gives you light.*

This Scripture, like many others in God's Word, has hidden spiritual meanings that provide instructions on how to have healthy insides—thoughts and emotions. Let me attempt to translate in two different ways to drive home the meaning. Note: I make no assertion of being a theologian, just a mom trying to make it simple.

My first interpretation of Luke 11:34-36: What you watch and take into your mind determines how bright your light shines. When you watch things that are fueled by the kingdom of darkness, you will not feel well. Remember, the heavenly Father lives in you so you can have joy, peace, and righteousness. If you don't, it could be because of something you saw.

OK, here's another way of saying Luke 11:34-36: What your mind is pondering on can be determined by what you watch, which ultimately determines if you manifest the Kingdom of light (God; Jesus) versus the kingdom of darkness (satan, devil). Don't forget that since the mind of Christ lives within you, all of your ways should reflect His ways. If they don't, think about what you have been watching and stop what isn't godly and righteous.

Let's pause for some self-reflective questions:

- Do you know what your child daydreams about? (Yes or No)
- Do you ask? (Yes or No)
- Do you know what movies and television shows he/she may be really in to? (Yes or No) If no, it's time to find out.

Mass Media Is a Major Mountain

Media is one of the "seven mountains of cultural influence," along with business, government, entertainment, family, education, and religion. Social media is a major vehicle being used to carry the kingdom of darkness culture. Over a period of time, it can chip away at the convictions we try to cultivate in our children.

More and more television shows and commercials are introducing alternative lifestyles, such as homosexuality, as an acceptable way to live. The more you see it, the more common and acceptable it becomes.

As these seed-like ideologies enter into the hearts and minds of our children, we find that they begin to rage up against the mind of their maker, God. We must not continue as parents to allow television, social media, iPods, and 21st century culture to indoctrinate, parent, or babysit our children. We must exercise our God-given authority in love to guide them toward the Kingdom of Heaven.

Telling them no may not good be enough, we have to be educated and empowered enough to explain why.

The Wolves at the Gates

Guarding their gates is a weapon. You may be familiar with the saying, "Wolves in sheep clothing," but what about: cartoon networks in sheep clothing; musical lyrics in sheep clothing; educational systems in sheep clothing; clothing lines in sheep clothing; Disney movies in sheep clothing; television shows in sheep clothing; social media in sheep clothing; and books in sheep clothing?

Reading all of this you may be overwhelmed and think, *"Man, we can't do anything,"* or some may think, *"We can't tackle all that, what's the big deal,"* or *"This is too over-the-top and downright religious."* My answer to that parent is that it only takes a little leaven to leaven the whole lump (Galatians 5:9). Even though this particular verse in the Bible refers to false teachings and doctrines spreading through the Body of Christ, the premise still applies because all doctrines, ways, beliefs, and actions that are not of God can be placed in the false teaching category. All of the areas that are listed are factual, proven areas known to carry dark agendas such as witchcraft, voodoo, homosexuality, gender confusion, same sex marriage, occultism, and sexual perversion; just to name a few. All of which are completely opposite to living in the Kingdom of God.

I feel some readers may be a little annoyed because I may have placed one of their sacred cows in the wolves in sheep clothing category. The first one that comes to mind is Disney. Just so that they don't remain offended and miss the whole point of using this book to empower their child, let's jump right into investigating Disney and the messages being sent through movies.

Please do your own investigation; but while performing mine, I could not find one Disney movie that does not include some kind of voodoo, sorcery, witchcraft, sexually charged, or mature relationship concepts. Why does a three-year-old need to see two cartoons kissing? Why does a five-year-old need to learn how to cast spells? If the presentation was not cartoonish and colorfully filled with cool songs, parents would naturally think twice about putting young children in front of it.

Disney has done a great job in making evil appear "not that dark or scary." Would you let your young child watch *Annabelle, Child's Play,* or the *Exorcist?* You more than likely would say, "Heck no," but the same source that created those dark evil films created the ones on many of the cartoon networks that parents let babysit and entertain their kids. My question is, "Why are parents doing that?"

The word "entertain" is defined by Merriam Webster's dictionary as *"to keep, to hold, or maintain in the mind."* With this understanding, what are parents allowing to infiltrate the minds of their children while they are being held and maintained? Christian parents who believe in *"whatever is true, whatever is noble, whatever is right, whatever is pure, whatever is lovely, whatever is admirable—if anything is excellent or praiseworthy—think about such things"* (Philippians 4:8 NIV), should seriously consider monitoring what their children see—and think about.

Parental Warning!

OK, back to Disney. The cartoons that they are pushing appear to be parentally acceptable only because they added color; but they can paint it red and white, add black ears, and call it a mouse, but at the end of the day, it's still witchcraft and sorcery. Go ahead, it's OK to say, "Ouch." I know that one really hurt because Mickey Mouse *is* very cute, that's why he perfectly fits into one of my wolves in sheep clothing boxes. Sorry to be the one to break it to you, but Mickey Mouse is a cutely drawn sorcerer.

The grand idea is to desensitize us into believing that it's OK to watch this kind of innocent "entertainment"; but the Bible is very clear about not indulging in spells, divination, and witchcraft. Yet we put our kids in front of it for hours on end completely unaware of how it's influencing their hearts or what doors are being cracked open to a dark world that would love to have your child on its side.

Galatians 5:19-20 (NIV) says, *"The acts of the flesh are obvious: sexual immorality, impurity and debauchery; idolatry and witchcraft; hatred, discord, jealousy, fits of rage, selfish ambition, dissensions, factions."*

By continuing to allow your children, if this applies to you, to be exposed to behaviors that the Bible classifies as *"acts of the flesh,"* you may be feeding a desire in them that one day could become out of their control because of an unlawful infiltration. I can 100 percent say that I could not afford that gamble—the cost would be too much if I lost.

Disobedience is Risky

A frequently used way the enemy is allowed to infiltrate our lives and homes is by our disobedience and rebellion. Since we are the guardians of our children, unfortunately our decisions not only affect us but they affect the kids, the fish, and the dog.

Selah Moment—aka Pause and Think

I know this chapter is full of a lot of information, so let's take a moment to reflect. If you find yourself at this point saying, "Yes, I'm one of those parents who have exposed my kids to some of the areas on the wolves in sheep clothing list. What do I do now?" This is where God's grace comes in. Right at this moment you can change the way you think, close some open doors, and educate yourself on what is capturing the eye and ear gates of your children. If what you learn doesn't line up to biblical standards, begin explaining and training your kids why they can no longer do x, y, and z.

Please Call Housekeeping

You may also want to do some housecleaning and invite your child along on this journey. This can be not only a bonding moment but an empowering one for your child to kick out of the house things that are attached to the wolves in sheep clothing list.

How can this be communicated to a child who is of age to better understand? Let's take a look at how I often go about it with my younger two girls.

Conversation Example 1

Hey _____ (insert child's name), I want to chat with you about some things that I just learned and I would love to get your thoughts on it. I was reading in the Bible that God really doesn't want for us to play with things like magic, voodoo, or casting spells. Did you know that?

Q. Do you know why?

A. Because all three of those things are games that the enemy or the devil created. (If necessary, take your time to make sure your child fully understands this concept before moving on.)

Q. What games should we play with? God games or devil games?

Take some time to explain the best way you can on how devil games equate to magic, voodoo, spell games, etc. Feel free to use the "A few words explained" resource in the back of the book.

Hopefully they say, "God games," but if they do not, don't panic. Now it's time to listen, learn, and better understand who the devil is to them, and why they would choose the devil over God games.

Assuming they chose God games, let's move on with the conversation: "Now, that we both agree that God games are the ones we should play, after doing some research, I found that there are some television shows and movies that have devil games in them. Do you know which ones might have devil games?" Many kids already have a hunch when things don't feel right, so their answers may actually surprise you.

"Do you remember what I said about God not being happy with us when we watch or play with those games? Well, what do you think we should do about those shows (or activities) we have been watching or playing?"

Attempt to get the child to assert and agree they should not be watching or playing them. This is also a good time to say, "I apologize for exposing you to these things, I promise in the future to be more careful, but I'm going to need your help with that. Could you tell me anytime you think you're watching something that's not good or are around a devil game?" You would be surprised to know that kids are more aware of these things than they may communicate or let on.

Congratulations! Now you both are investigators! Nine out of ten times the child is excited about feeling empowered to share. I have to say that in the beginning it may be over the top but indulge and affirm their ability to be able to now spot darkness when they see it.

Funny Story

During the time I was writing this book, my two youngest daughters were seven and eight, but right around the ages of five and six, we allowed them to be part of our "watch out for" conversations with their older two siblings. During this particular season, my two older kids were doing an investigation on the subliminal messaging hidden in musical lyrics, videos, and clothes.

Our study led us to several artists who, by watching their videos, they could clearly see their connection to satanism. This included ritualistic dark behaviors with underlining usages of the "all-seeing eye (refer to the "A few words explained" guide for more understanding)," with hand gestures creating pyramids, and so forth. It was so over the top that all, and I mean all, made some kind of triangle shape hand gesture, image, or pyramid.

One night my five-year-old was doing her homework and she came running through the house yelling "Mommy, mommy, my homework is a part of the Loominati." She clearly meant, Illuminati. Anyway, I was like, "What!? Let me see." I grabbed her sheet and very quickly saw what she was talking about. She had to group various shapes together and one of the shapes just happened to be a triangle. I'm not going to lie, we all laughed out loud on that one, but I realized she was at least paying attention. Of course, there will be times when you have to level set and explain, maybe even clarify, that triangles are not bad, but training their discernment and awareness early on will pay off later.

The Enemy Can't Create So He Steals

I say this to my kids a lot, "The enemy stinks at creating from scratch." The enemy is not a creator, he is an imitator and a thief. He takes the good that God made and uses it for his own purposes, he loves to pervert the uses of God's creation. This concept helps children better understand that even though the enemy may be using something as simple as an eye or triangle for a message, that does not mean we can't draw them.

A most recent topic in my house was the rainbow. My daughter told me that she's not going to wear her pretty rainbow shirt any more. I knew the answer, but asked her why anyway. She responded, "I don't want anyone to think I'm supporting the LGBTQ agenda."

So I asked her, "When you think of a rainbow, what's the first thing that comes to mind?" She very quickly said, "A few things. It's pretty, after it rains it's so cool to see in the sky, and of course Noah's ark." I told her this is a great example of beautiful, godly symbolism being snatched and repurposed for ungodliness. I then told her if someone asked her about it, simply share what it means to you and move on. This response not only allowed for her to stand up for what she believed in but it gave her permission to wear a shirt she really likes. My goal is not to be bullied by the enemy or his tactics.

OK, now let's review a potential conversation that could take place after you have had the first conversation and the child has a good foundation.

Follow-Up Conversation

Hi _____ *(insert child's name)*. I wanted to chat with you about the Halloween party you were invited to at your school. I know when you gave me the invitation you sounded like you really wanted to go. Is that true? (If the response is yes, you can proceed.)

Remember a little while ago we had a conversation about God games and devil games? (Hopefully the child remembers, but if not, go back to conversation 1.)

Well, Halloween fits into the wolves in sheep clothing bucket and it's a not a God game—it's a devil game. Do you know where Halloween came from? (If the response is no, make it a teaching moment. Under the "A few words explained" section, you will find a brief description on Halloween and why we should not participate. You can use this template for anything including movies, television shows, books, games, events, and outings.)

For years and years millions worldwide including Christians followed the Harry Potter series craze. They loved it, followed it, and allowed their children to be entertained by it—despite its very clear foundational premise of witchcraft and sorcery. Recently a Catholic school removed Harry Potter books from their school library citing them dangerous for housing "real spells." What that school failed to realize is that the book was already unlawful whether the spells were real or not. Any book that is given over to necromancy, sorcery, witchcraft, and divination should be placed 100 percent in the DO NOT TOUCH devil game bucket.

Setting Standards Without Compromise

Parent, we have to set standards for our children that are clear and without compromise.

Let's say you created something and then sprinkled it in the world with the understanding that whoever has it also provides you an open-door policy to come into their house without a key at any time. Now, with that being said, when we invite things into our home that belong to the enemy, or are authored by him, he says, "Now I have a legal right to come and go as I please in your home."

You have to get your kids to understand that there are always strings attached to the devil games. My prayer is that you will throw away every object, book, movie, video, perspective, and conversation that are dueling as undercover keys of access in the hearts and minds of you and your child.

Make the great exchange from ungodly to godly and set the standard that your home will be a place where only light reigns. Where peace, love, hope, faith, and joy live. And where anxiety, fear, condemnation, self-hatred, and torment are not permitted to enter—ever.

But, Why?

The following are a few questions that you as a parent should be ready to immediately answer if your child asks you:

- Why should I *not* play with an Ouija board?
- Why should I *not* watch horror movies?

▪ Why should I be careful about what games I play and what music I listen to?

Typically, generation X (born 1965-1980) parents are raising Millennials and Generation Zs and information is readily available and at their fingertips all day long. These children are taught very different from past generations such as Baby Boomers (born 1944-1964).

Gen Xers were semi-okay with being told what to do, not 100% understanding why, but Millennials and Generation Zs are taught from a young age to challenge theory, ask why, challenge ideas, and critically think. These ways of learning, at the core, are not evil and are extremely helpful in solving many of life's problems. The challenge we face now as parents is that we cannot feed our children lines like, "Just don't do it." We should be empowering them with biblical truths to better understand the "why" behind our decisions. This model loads them up with crucial information that will build a foundation for them to stand on for years to come.

We cannot not give them a religion based on traditions resulting in no power to face life's challenges. We must follow the example of Christ and give them biblical truths that are supported by Jesus's Gospel of demonstration. Just do what I say with no demonstration is no longer going to hold their hearts captive.

Our children are a generation that need true and real relationship and God encounters. They need to hear God for themselves; they need to know and experience the guidance of the Holy Spirit in their lives; they want and were created to walk in authority;

they want to be the head and not the tail; and they want to experience the God of the Bible.

The good news about this realization is that they can have all of that. As Bible-believing parents, we do not have to leave our children wanting and longing for something that actually does exist. The Word of God is complete with the what, when, why, where, and how of connecting with the Father. It's the best Book ever written because it unveils the mind of our Maker. It unravels God's thoughts toward His creation, His promises, who we are, and what He has planned for us. If you have not done so already, I invite you as a child overseer to fall in love with the Word of God. In Chapter Eight, we will dig deeper into this very topic because the Word is a weapon.

Your Ears are a Gate

Several years ago there was a hit song that made it to #1 for weeks and weeks on the billboard charts titled *Roar,* by Katy Perry. I heard everyone singing this song, in the church and out of the church, even my kids were in love with this song. We chose as a family not to listen to the popular secular songs on the radio by well-known secular artists like Jay Z, Beyoncé, 50 cent, Lady Gaga, and so on; but because my kids do not live on an island by themselves, they hear music everywhere.

Knowing this, it was my mission to educate and empower them to learn how to guard their own ear gates. They have been raised to investigate before they "dive in" or allow anything to entertain, aka enter into them. With that in mind, my ten-year-old daughter at the time asked, "Mom, what do you think about the song *Roar* by Katy Perry?" I love these kinds of questions from my children because to be honest, when I was their age, I just snuck around and did things despite my parent's discouragement to do so. Being invited on a journey to find out the "why" is one of the best compliments a parent could ever get.

Later that evening, we sat down together and our investigation began. As worship leaders ourselves, my children have been taught and are well aware of song writing, atmospheres, and the power that music has. While performing song investigations, we don't jump right into the lyrics, we first search out the writers. Who are they, what are their values, morals, agendas, etc.?

"Why?" you may ask. Glad you asked, because the answers to those type of questions will provide insight into what's in their spirit. While listening to music composed by someone, it's important for you to know that what is in them will infiltrate you, both good and bad. That's why if you're a worship leader, it's crucial to live at the feet of the Father so that as He gets in you, when you pour out, it's Him.

OK, back to the investigation. It didn't take long before we stumbled on a YouTube video of Katy Perry telling her story. She began to share that both of her parents were ministers, she grew up in a Christian home, and when she was fifteen years old, she wrote a song about her story. She then went on to talk about how she wanted to be the next Amy Grant, but that didn't work out so she sold her soul to the devil. Now I have never had a conversation with Katy Perry to fully dive into what that really meant for her, but that statement was enough for my daughter to say, "Thanks, but no thanks."

Why? Kristian understands that music is a vehicle used to deliver messages. Music creates atmospheres; and while listening to it, you are brought into an encounter determined by the spirit and intentions of the writer, composer and or the singer. Music has the power to alter people's emotions and thinking. With this understanding, it highlights a great need to investigate the music you and your children listen to. No matter what words are being sung, music is a special, unexplainable experience that has the ability to impose the writer's spirit into the listener's spirit.

Atmospheres 101

Regarding atmosphere and music, have you ever been part of a worship service and the worship leaders are singing all the "right" songs, their hands are lifted, their eyes may even be closed, and everything from a natural perspective appears to be in order—but for some reason your spirit just doesn't agree or you may even feel vexed?

I believe that people can only give what they have or carry. If they are full of God's presence, mind, hope, love, joy, and peace, then that is what will flow from them into the atmosphere they are called to influence. If a person is bound, frustrated, hopeless, fearful, etc., then no matter what they say or sing, those attributes are what will be released into the atmosphere. This concept does not change based on the style of music—it holds true for all. Understanding the spirit of the person you are opening yourself up to and using godly discernment is important to ensure your soul is not being negatively impacted.

After our investigation, I'm sure I don't have to say it, but my daughter never asked to listen to another Katy Perry song again.

Let's Go Fox Hunting

Song of Songs 2:15 (ESV) says, *"Catch the foxes for us, the little foxes that spoil the vineyards, for our vineyards are in blossom."*

It's time to uncover the little foxes and bind them up so they no longer are permitted to eat away at the fruit that was deposited into the hearts of our children. The goal is to close all open doors and remove the bullseye target on their backs, allowed to remain because of ignorance, disobedience, and even potentially curiosity.

I heard a quote by an unknown author that really helped explain music as a device that the enemy uses to permeate our children: "If you want to influence the minds of a generation, hide a doctrine in the music of that generation." This statement alone should make you want to investigate the songs and artists tucked away on your child's iPod or iPhone.

Prayer Declaration

Dear heavenly Father, I thank You for revealing to me that there are some areas in my child's life that need more of You. Guide me and give me the words to say to be able to better understand what is happening deep inside _____ (insert child's name). *Give me holy discernment and allow me to hear Your voice as we embark on the journey of allowing Your ways to go deeper into our hearts. Father, please expose any areas in our lives that we have opened up to the enemy. Give us grace and wisdom about how to walk in Your ways. In Jesus's name I pray, amen.*

Selah Moment

Let's pause for some self-reflective questions:

- Do you know what your child daydreams about? (Yes or No)
- Do you ask? (Yes or No)
- Do you know what movies and television shows your child really likes? (Yes or No)

If any of your answers were no, it's time to ask your child. Allow these questions to begin a deeper level journey to getting to know your child better.

Chapter Five

IDENTITY IS A WEAPON

Identity Crises

I believe it does not take a prophet or even a theologian to come up with the assertion that many people are suffering from identity crises in this day in age. Many are afraid to release their true authentic selves, so they emulate what appears to be accepted—and now we have a society of self-created clones.

Children get their self-confidence and identity from their parents, and even more specifically, their fathers. During biblical times it was the father who laid hands on the child and released destiny and blessings. When did this tradition stop? Is this the reason why many of the younger generations are blindly walking through life with no real sense of direction?

Parent, we must get back to the times when it was cool for parents to speak life into their kids. Do you know why God chose you specifically out of billions of other choices? Why would He choose you to be the tool of development for the little person you call son or daughter. One thing I do know is that the million-dollar question parents should be asking of God is, "Who am I raising, and why me?"

I know you may be thinking, *Why ask why, right?* Well, those answers are tied directly into what you are expected to impart into your child. It's the mission of all missions. If you don't know who you are raising, what their purpose is, and what are their gifts, could there be a major parental misfire with the way you're raising them? God knew that you were the best person for the job, whether you believe it or not. How we respond from there is something we will have to answer for.

DEAR PARENT, PLEASE UNDERSTAND THAT YOU ARE NOT RAISING AN ORPHAN BUT RATHER A KING.

We Are Raising Kings

Several territories in the world today are still classified as a kingdom that is being ruled by a king or queen. In those territories, when a child is born into the royal family they are groomed and trained from childbirth on how to be *"royal."* How to walk royal, how to think royal, how to behave royal. They are instructed on how to respond in a royal manner and ultimately given a "royal" identity all because of their royal bloodline.

"But you are a chosen people, a royal priesthood, a holy nation, God's special possession, that you may declare the praises of him who called you out of darkness into his wonderful light." (1 Peter 2:9 NIV)

We Too Have Royalty in Our Bloodline

As a result of the work of the cross and what Jesus did for us, we too have been adopted into a royal family. The Scriptures teach us that the God is King of kings (Revelations 19:16; Deuteronomy 10:17). The second king in that particular Scripture is referencing us, His children. God said in Genesis that He has given us dominion and authority over the earth and all the works of His hands (Genesis 1:26). If we begin to instill in our children that they too are born into a royal family and they themselves can rule and reign as a king in the earth, they then will begin to respond and make decisions for their lives from a higher level of thinking, a royal one.

It is crucial to the success of our children that we teach them who they are in Christ and what has been appropriated to them in order for them to come into the fullness of who they are created to be. My prayer is that our children's identity will be anchored in the value that has been given to them by their father God and believe that anything opposite of that is a lie.

Identity Can Be Found in Their Calling

Are you raising a prophet or a pastor? You may not be raising either, but it's extremely crucial for you to find out. Why? I believe there are certain gifts that draw out different levels of attack from the kingdom of darkness, such as prophets.

Opinion disclaimer: Please note that the previous assertion is completely from my own personal observations and experiences; I am not quoting as a concrete biblical doctrine.

What I can say that is biblical about prophets is that they have spiritual X-ray vision to see, uncover, and uproot the plans of the enemy. More importantly, though, their ears are spiritually tuned to simply hear the voice of their God. Healthy ones are intolerant of injustice toward God's people, communities, and themselves. Their principle-driven nature has the potential to unnerve those who live life on the balance beam called compromise.

Raising prophets takes parents who can skillfully develop maturity into the heart of this principled, justice-driven child. As children, prophets need a lot of love sown into their hearts. Affirmation of their identity and value is so important to build a foundation that they later will need to stand on. Scripture is very clear that *"Out of the mouth of babes...thou has perfected praise"* (Matthew 21:16 KJV). Being young is not an excuse to ignore the gifts lying dormant inside your child.

God said to Jeremiah, "Say not that I am a child"; and even though Jeremiah's assignment was one of the hardest, being sent to a stubborn rebelling generation, being young still did not let him off the hook. With this understanding, we still cannot ignore that there is a process of development for every gift, even Jesus went through a thirty-year process for a three-year ministry. One thing we can find in Scripture is that Jesus did not waste time even as a child. Although young, He was found ministering in the temples and spending time with the Father—a lifestyle forged in Him way before adulthood.

An interesting concept about Jesus's first miracle that connects to parental involvement is that His mother is the one who pushed Him into turning water into wine. She knew exactly who He was and what He could do. There was no doubt in her mind that her Son was created to solve problems. She knew that if there was a problem, He was there to solve it.

Do you know what your child is capable of or what problem he or she was created to solve?

A Letter to My Son

With permission from my sixteen-year-old son, I want to share with you a letter I wrote to him. I am only sharing because my prayer is that my transparency with my son will expose the journey we are on together—him seeking to find his place in the world, who he is and why he was created. My letter reminds him of what's important and attempts to refocus him on seeking his life mission. If we can get our kids thinking this way well before adulthood, they should have a head start on crucial life questions that many individuals well into their thirties and forties are just beginning to ask.

Dear Kamryn,

I'm writing this letter because many times verbal words get processed too fast, so I figure if I WRITE this very important message, you will be forced to stare at every word to process it. My prayer is that as you stare at it, each word will sink deep down, so deep you really truly believe it.

YOU, my son, are here on earth for a purpose, more than likely to solve a problem. A family problem, a community problem, a culture problem, a political problem, or maybe even a spiritual problem; nevertheless, you are not here just simply to take up space. Your first mission is not to make the basketball team, graduate H.S. or even find who your next girlfriend is. Your mission is to find out what problem you were created to solve. Once you have that answer, you more than likely may have just found your purpose.

Once you have purpose and you become excited to fulfill it, you will then realize that nothing is worth detouring from it. You will find that the minor temptations that will come your way will not compare to the gratification of solving that problem. Because you are so gifted, it may be easy to inaccurately identify a problem as "the one," but listen to the Holy Spirit because He will validate it for you. Stop caring about what people think. Stop living your life in-jailed by the small opinions of others. Stop being afraid to fail. Stop believing the lie that you don't measure up. Think big, live big, and do not be scared to make mistakes trying to solve "that problem."

I love you with all that is within me. Now go out and complete the mission and solve "that problem."

Love,

Mom, your biggest fan

Now that I have been awakened to the concept that it's important to know who we're raising, I am so aware of who my children are and pay very close attention to how they maneuver through life.

Raising four children, I honestly have been given a front row seat into many of the ministry gifts—apostle, prophet, pastor, teacher, and evangelist (Ephesians 4:11)—and other gifts as well. I didn't always understand, so hopefully you can learn from my missteps.

Break-in news flash! There is no big Holy Spirit for adults and little Holy Spirit for children. I really like how Pastor Bill Johnson says it, "There is no Junior Holy Spirit for kids." What I have come to realize is that our children have the ability to house in them the same Spirit who raised Jesus from the dead. He desires to express His character, likeness, and power through your child. Wow, if only I knew how special I was as a child! Let's make sure our children know so they are set up to be all they can be through Christ.

Story Time

Shock face was my reaction when my five-year-old tapped my hand in service and said "Mom, I have something to say to the people," while motioning for the microphone. This particular Sunday was my time to open the service for worship. As I was looking through my Bible for an opening Scripture that would make ready the hearts of God's people, I kept being distracted by seeing my five-year-old walking around with a pencil and paper chatting with not necessarily everyone but very specific individuals. I couldn't hear what she was saying, but at a glance it didn't seem like people were bothered, so I permitted this childlike game to continue.

When she was finished, she came over and sat directly next to me and said, "God told me to say something to the people." I have to apologize in advance because my first reaction was not, "Well bless the name of the Lord. As soon as I'm done opening, I'll give you the microphone, honey."

Rather, I bent down, chuckled a little, and said, "Are you serious?" She had the biggest grin ever and said, "Yes, I need to say something to the people." At first, I honestly patronized the situation and thought for sure that when I "act like" I'm going to hand her the microphone, she will run off laughing, and whatever this was will be over.

I know what you're thinking, *Why would a mother, especially a spiritual one, respond this way?* Where's my faith, right? Well, you have to understand, Moriah has never done this before or even shown interest in releasing a prophetic declaration. All my kids have been exposed to teachings and trainings on hearing the voice of God; but to be honest, she was getting trickled down lessons because at that time I was really focusing on activating the older two.

Anyway, back to the story.

The clock struck six o'clock and it was go time. I stood up, and so did Moriah. I walked to the front, and so did Moriah. I opened with reading a great Scripture passage and exhortation, and the people appeared to be all set and ready for service to begin. I took a short glance downward to see what Moriah's posture was, only a mom can detect a fear or flight response coming—and what I saw was strength and determination.

After giving her a brief introduction and gently prepping the people to receive, "God only knows what," I slowly handed her the microphone. She grabbed the microphone and in her five-year-old voice she said, "God said, He loves you very much." Then she held up a piece of paper and announced, "He said to tell you that He knows your name." Little did I know that when she was walking around earlier, she was going to specific people and writing their names on that same piece of paper she held up high. She continued to say, "He also said go to the park, it's time to have some fun."

She closed her prophetic encouragement by saying, "OK, that's it, goodbye," giggled and ran off. Once I managed to pick my jaw up from the floor, I lifted my head to see several individuals weeping and extremely touched at how the Father's love just flowed through a five-year-old little girl with cookie crumbs on her cheeks. I'll say it again, it's important to know who you are raising. From that moment on, my heart was so humbled and ready to train her in her weapon, prophecy.

Who Are You Raising?

Who are your kids? Do you know who you are raising? Do you know their spiritual gifts and callings? Why were they created? What was God thinking when He called them into existence? Whose lives will be impacted simply because they were born? Why are you their parent? What did God see in you that would be crucially necessary to ensure you were their parent? These are just some of the questions I have asked myself over the years while raising my children.

> *Children are a heritage from the Lord, offspring a reward from him. Like arrows in the hands of a warrior are children born in one's youth. Blessed is the man whose quiver is full of them. They will not be put to*

shame when they contend with their opponents in court (Psalm 127:3-5 NIV).

There are so many Scriptures in the Bible that fortify how blessed we are to be raising children. Be encouraged to thank God every day for the children He has so graciously entrusted to you.

May Your Quiver Be Full

Many years ago, I was at an amazing worship conference hosted by a wonderful ministry called, The Blessing Place. There were so many times at those conferences that through prophecy God confirmed Himself to us, provided instructions, strategies, and even at times rebukes. During this particular conference, I received the latter, a rebuke. After the service was over, like many other times in the past, people never wanted to leave. We would just hang out in the presence of God getting downloads directly from the voice of God.

A gentleman we knew at the time came over to my husband and myself and said, "Do you mind if I share with you a word that I believe the Father is downloading for you two?" I was so excited. I'm one who loves prophecy and hearing God's love being spoken over me, so I remember assuming the position. You probably know what I mean—arms out, palms up and open.

He began to share about God's love for us and expounded on the provision of Heaven being our portion, and how the Father was pleased with our worship, and was so proud of us. Then he continued and shared, "God desires for our quiver to be full." That's when I broke the position. *Quiver? Full? Wait, ain't that a lot of kids?* I know the man couldn't hear my thoughts, so it must have been by facial expressions that clearly vexed him, because he stopped and looked at me and said, "Do you know what quiver means?" I said, "Yes, I know what it means. Your home or womb will be full of a lot of kids, right?"

Let me explain why I broke position. During that time, I really did not want to have any more children. I was content with the two we had and our finances, as well as our marriage, were being challenged on all sides. The thought of bringing more children into the world honestly overstressed me and simply was not something I desired. I expressed this concern to him and my statement appeared to shoot out like an arrow into his heart because he burst into a violent cry. I just stared at him and was wondering why me not wanting more kids bothered him so much. I just stood there waiting to gain more understanding.

He finally gathered himself long enough to preach a message I will never forget. He began to share that it was very hard for him to be asked by God to give words of babies coming to people because he never knew what that was like. You see, he never was able to father any natural children, which was a deep desire of his. He was now well into his sixties, but the river of tears showed that, like apostle Paul, he had a thorn in his flesh that would not be removed.

He continued to share that children are blessings from God and they are an inheritance. I finally relented in my heart to allow for him to continue. He concluded our encounter by prophesying about the children that we had yet to conceive. After wiping away the tears, we hugged, and I left with a seeded desire in my heart to now know the children that this man so boldly spoke about under the influence of the Holy Spirit.

Some of my most beautiful life moments have been shared with my four children and I cannot imagine life without even one of them. I cherish each of them and completely adore them. It pains my heart to even think of them going through tough times, but a revelation that I have come to understand is that God only lent them to me for His purpose; and ultimately, they really are His.

Psalm 127 speaks about children being a reward from the Lord. Back in Bible days, the more children you had, the more "blessed" you were. Children were wealth, they were not just something to take care of, but more of a blessed line to leave your inheritance through so they could spread and cover the earth by carrying your name.

> *Behold, children are a heritage from the Lord, the fruit of the womb is a reward. Like arrows in the hand of a warrior, so are the children of one's youth* (Psalm 127:3-4 NKJV).

When you as a parent begin to raise your children according to who the Father designed them to be, you now are using the blueprints of Heaven to partner as a special architect and engineer. Your love and your discipline now have another level of purpose, versus this is what I should and am expected to do. Every hug is a seed of affirmation. Every word of affirmation is a counterattack to a seed of rejection the enemy will eventually use against them one day. Every moment of playing games and spending quality time is an atomic bomb being launched into the camp of spies seeking an open door of abandonment. With children as part of your family, everything in life has a deeper level of intention and passion. I ask you again, do you know who you birthed or are raising?

Here Comes Rebuke Number Two

I will shamefully say that I received a total of three rebukes connecting to having more children, this next one is rebuke number two. We just completed a Sunday service and were sitting around chatting with our pastors at the time. We spoke about the service, how great the word was and how we were doing as a family. A question was asked of us, very nonchalantly, "Do you guys want more kids?" Now this conversation was unique for me because I knew that the pastor's wife had one child, and at that time was not able to conceive another. Knowing this, I was on guard and chose my words very carefully, not wanting to offend them in any way.

I very strategically and lightly stated, "We're OK with the two we have." We had a boy and a girl at home, which did not include my bonus three stepchildren, another reason why at that time I was simply, "OK." The pastor's wife looked at me and said, "It's not about you being 'OK,' it's about who you are birthing in the earth. They will be giant slayers." Then she just walked off. That was yet another drop-the-mic moment in my life, connecting to God's desire for us to have more children. Now that I have them, I completely understand why, because they truly are giant killers.

I ask you again, do you know who you are raising—*identity for your child will be a weapon.*

Guard Your Children's Hearts

But whoso shall offend one of these little ones which believe in me, it were better for him that a millstone were hanged about his neck, and that he were drowned in the depth of the sea (Matthew 18:6 KJV).

Wait, does this Scripture include me and my kids too? This verse honestly scared me when I first read it, because all parents know that at some point in a parenting journey, they are going to "offend" their kids. The first time you tell them no or make the dinner they really didn't want, an offense will shortly follow. After studying this Scripture verse a little deeper, I came to understand that the offense in that verse had nothing to do with godly disciplining your child. The word "offend" comes from the Greek word *skandalizo*. I know what you're thinking, *That word looks a lot like scandalize.* If you caught that, you're on to something.

Author Remix Coming Right Up

Sharee's paraphrase: Whoever causes a scandal in the life of a child big enough to cause them to turn away (apostatize) from ever desiring to know Me (Jesus), they will be oh so sorry and most certainly regret the outcome.

Now do you understand the importance and necessity of giving our children the truth of God's Word, love, training, and protection? We are held accountable as entrusted guardians in their lives; held accountable for our actions toward them and what we seed into them. We cannot hypocritically proclaim a loving God as our own—and at the same time demonstrate hell in the home.

> *The King will reply, "Truly I tell you, whatever you did for one of the least of these brothers and sisters of mine, you did for me"* (Matthew 25:40 NIV).

Let's explore the idea that loving our kids is loving God. When I finally decided to have more children, they came very quickly. My last two children are exactly twelve months apart and my fourth was conceived after my tubes were tied; that one is our little Moriah I spoke about earlier in the chapter. With them being only twelve months apart, I felt like I was so exhausted for almost four years straight. To be honest, everything was such a chore, including at times taking care of them. I know it was God's grace that got me through those times, but there was also another revelation that pulled me through—I knew that what I was doing for them I was doing for the Father as well.

Every diaper, every night I walked the floor singing over them, every time I spoke kind words to them, every cup of water given, and every peanut butter and jelly sandwich made was as if I was making it for my heavenly Father. I remember looking at them, asking the Father, "Who are they?" In those moments, He opened His heart to share what He was dreaming when they were created. He spoke over each one. One a prophet, another a teacher, missionary, singer, musician, and so on. Once I was armed with who they were, even though this concept was new to me, I still somehow knew that I needed to raise them according to "who God ordained them to be" versus what my husband and I thought would be cool.

I paid close attention to their personalities, dispositions, weaknesses, and their strengths. I watched and still do watch their enthusiasm for spiritual things or lack thereof. I made mental notes of the ones who were drawn to the spirit realm versus the why factor sometimes mirroring apologetics. All of this information aids in building strategies on how to train and raise up children for God's glory.

Why is all of that even important? I'm glad you asked. I never will forget the time my son was around four years old. It was breakfast time and he looked so sad. He was gazing out the kitchen window not eating his cereal, which was a major red flag. I remember asking him, "Kam, what's wrong?" He lifted his head and said, "Mom, movers are coming, the boxes are here." Panic shot through my heart because this house was like our dream house, we were not even there two full years.

I dismissed his statement and said, "Kam, no, we just moved here, that's probably why you're seeing movers." Saying that only appeased the moment; deep within I felt like what he saw was a heads-up, or a get ready. Well, it wasn't even six months later when we were forced to sell our dream home because of losing my job in the mortgage industry during the banking industry bust.

Prophets as children may possibly resemble the child who may always have a lot of dreams and they just seem to, for some reason, come true. The ministry gift does not discriminate against age; they are who they are from the womb. They cannot help it and as previously stated, they will prophesy even if it's by accident. Now that I am aware of the concept that it's important to know who you're raising, I am so on guard of who they are and pay very close attention to how they maneuver through life.

I love to watch my children as they are growing into who they will be. Seeing their gifts work even while playing with one another is amazing. I can detect the child who has the gift of administration putting order in the room, and the one who operates in mercy become a defender of the weak. There's the one who feels rejected if I dare tell her not to set the table. Her gift of helps would just melt like butter. With this understanding, I now say no very carefully and strategically.

When my daughter was young, I stepped on her sensitive nature so many times I can't even give you a number. She was the child who did not want me to do anything on my own. If she was around, she was going to try to help get it done. I will never forget the time Kristian asked me to help with a household chore. Like many parents feel, at the time I honestly just wanted to be finished and move on to the next task. I knew if at that moment I allowed her to join in, it would only slow me down, so I simply said, "No, not right now," and kept it moving.

When I came back to the room where the conversation took place, I witnessed a meltdown like no other. Tears were streaming down Kristian's face, and her posture was of one who was broken and rejected. I truly didn't understand what happened, so I ran over to her and said, "Kris, what's wrong?" I was not prepared for her answer. She looked up at me, wiped her tears away with her sleeve, and said, "You won't let me help you." *Gasp! What!?*

At the time, I didn't understand why she reacted that way and I honestly felt at first it was some form of manipulation until I heard that still small voice say, "She has the gift of helps. Telling her no she can't help is like murdering one of her reasons to exist. It's part of the core of who she is."

Many times, we don't understand why our children react the way they do, we may even call it overreacting; but if the core of who you are was not given an opportunity to bloom or breathe, wouldn't you have a meltdown too?

After that revelation, I provided her opportunities to bloom and empowered her about the gift she carried. I allowed her to exist and simply be. Since I understand the weaknesses and strengths of that gift, I taught her how valued and appreciated she is. I taught her that she cannot do things for people just so they will like her or value her more, which can be another weakness. I also shared that she must use discernment to know when enough is enough and when she is being taken advantage of, something that happens many times with individuals with this gift.

This is just one of Kristian's spiritual gifts, but I find it to be a great example. Hopefully this story was a seed to cause you to explore and raise your children according to who they are designed to be and cultivate from there.

You're Not an Orphan

Encouraging our children to believe they have a heavenly Father who loves them despite what they've done or the mistakes they've made is powerful. Belonging and identity are weapons against the strategies that the enemy will attempt to use against them.

I was bullied in high school—all four years. As I look back, I remember that the first three years were bad, but not as bad as the fourth one. While pondering on the why, I was able to come to a conclusion. During the first three years of high school, one of my two older sisters were attending the same high school. Even though I was bullied, there was still something reassuring know-ing that I had some form of family support; and if necessary, I knew one of them would jump in. I suppose my bullies knew that as well. Knowing I belonged to a family who was present provided a layer of security and protection.

After both my sisters had graduated and I was left alone, I no longer had my security blankets, known also by those who sought to crush me. I'm also sure that my insecure posture was equal to spilling blood in an ocean of sharks sending a she's an easy target, come get her message. After my sisters were gone, I was simply fair game to the bullies. Just like there is an unwritten law that people can be "guilty by association," there is a spiritual law that says, "Victory is inevitable because of whose you are." When you're a child of the King, your victory is secure.

Rejection Is a Tool The Enemy Uses

Being in the deliverance ministry and ministering to people over many years, I have seen very similar trends that cause open doors to greater levels of bondage. One is *unforgiveness,* and the second is *rejection,* living with the orphan spirit. Many adults we minister to are still trying to get over childhood pains caused by their father or mother. I'm sure if the parents of those adults had a book like this, they may have done things differently; but the fact of the matter is, you can only do better if you know better.

With the understanding that rejection is a major tool the enemy uses against our children, I constantly pursue my children's hearts to get a better understanding of what's in there. I ask them, "Do you feel loved? Are you getting enough quality time with Dad and me?" There were a lot of times when their answers were not in my husband and my favor. You must be OK with that, partner with the Holy Spirit, and fix it.

Everyone in the world wants to know they are loved, wanted, and needed. What makes your child any different? They are searching for a place to not just take up space, but conquer their world and be noticed for the individuals they are. Don't forget that way back during creation days, God gave us all dominion over the works of His hands. Your children were born with this innate desire to "lord" over something. Like God, they want to create;

they need space to produce and be appreciated. Not permitting this could cause long-lasting implications that will later need to be uprooted possibly even through deliverance.

Since this book focuses mostly on prevention, I encourage you to investigate this topic further with your child and the Holy Spirit. Do they feel like they belong? Do they feel isolated, unwanted, or unheard? If you don't know, ask them. Ask them what you can do to make them feel more accepted, wanted, and desired. These questions alone show them that they are valued enough for Mom or Dad to seek to understand and make changes. You will be surprised at the answers you will get. Remember, keep your game face on, partner with the Holy Spirit, and move on lovingly and gently.

Self-Value Is a Healthy Filter

A concept that I honestly did not learn until after I was an adult and living with a slew of regrettable decisions and actions was: "Living life from the filter that I have value and worth is a must." Younger children and teenagers, especially in this day and age, are seeking to walk heavy in the earth. Children who were raised with self-confidence and a healthy identity will make wiser and less self-damaging decisions because their filter is not, "I'm only doing this for someone to like or love me." This message speaks to my heart because some place in me as a child lacked confidence and identity.

I often found myself in very dark, less-than-desirable places because of the habit of compromising myself to be with people who validated and made me feel important. Building a strong understanding of belonging and forging the awareness of being a King's kid into the heart of a child will usurp the plans of the enemy. Many adults still have not mastered the idea of being an heir in God's Kingdom. Too many believers still have a filter of slave versus son or heir. It's a works mentality; and when you mess up, condemnation sets in and the cycle of repenting begins. For some, it never translates into a relationship with their heavenly Father that is birthed out of a Father's love affair with His children. Ponder over and over the revelation that you are loved, wanted, and needed. Take a moment and just think about that. Now, how can your child come into this same revelation because of your actions toward them?

Prayer Declaration

Father, I thank You for revealing to me that _____ (insert child's name) *is a gift from You. I desire to know what You were thinking when You created this child. Open up my heart to fully understand the gifts and calling on this child so that I can partner with You and the Holy Spirit in raising this gift You have given me.*

I declare that _____ (insert child's name) *will love You, seek You, and want to please You. I declare Your love over* _____ *'s (insert child's name) heart and mind. Teach me how to teach this child and love You through me. In Jesus's name I pray, amen.*

Points to Ponder

- Your children are gifts from God.
- They have gifts, spiritual gifts, and calls that need to be cultivated and nurtured even while they are young.
- Find out who you are raising.
- Allow for an atmosphere of making mistakes and learning.
- Unconditional love will love the hell out of them.
- Always let them know they have a place in the well of your heart.
- Help them to believe that there is nothing they can ever do to cause you to stop loving them.
- Remind them that they are loved and accepted no matter what.

Activation Activity: Let's Chat Questions

Refer to "Conversation Starter Tips" located at the back of the book. Feel free to be creative and add age-appropriate questions that allows for deeper levels of dialog and the exposure of what's really going on deep down in the heart of your child.

Chapter Six

HEARING GOD AS A CHILD

*A primary element of God's character
is that He is a communicator.*

I love how the late Dr. Myles Munroe describes the Kingdom of God. He states that the Bible is about three main things: A King, a Kingdom, and His kids. From the Garden of Eden until now, God has desired to have communion with His family—and we are part of that family. He desires to talk and relate to humanity on an individual, personal level, just as He did in the beginning of time with Adam and Eve.

Though the outcome of what happened in the Garden was not what God planned, His original intentions never changed. I believe as soon as He saw this whole Garden thing was not going to work out, He set the plan in motion to redeem His family back to being able to walk with Him during the *"cool of the day."*

Genesis 3:8 (KJV) tells us: *And they heard the voice of the Lord God walking in the garden in the cool of the day: and Adam and his wife hid themselves from the presence of the Lord God amongst the trees of the garden.*

God has not changed His mind or desire to fellowship and commune with us.

God's Voice Is a Weapon

One of our strongest weapons against the enemy as children of God is to be able to effectively hear the voice of our God speaking personally to us. Many believers need to be taught that God still speaks and that He desires to be known and heard by His children. His voice is the most important voice we will ever hear in our lives.

With that understanding, this chapter was constructed to give tools to equip parents to empower their children to hear the voice of God for themselves. This lesson is one of the most important life lessons a parent can ever teach their child starting at a young age.

> But the Lord said to me, "Do not say, 'I am too young.' You must go to everyone I send you to and **say whatever I command you**" (Jeremiah 1:7 NIV).

Theologians state that Jeremiah could have been anywhere between the age of thirteen and seventeen, but there are no age restrictions to hearing God's voice. Jeremiah was just a young boy when God called him to be a prophet to the nations; and when Jeremiah gave God a legitimate excuse about being too young, it was quickly shot down. This Scripture not only sets a precedent for our children in removing the limits of what they spiritually can do, it also clearly identifies God's voice being present in a child's life.

According to Jewish historians, Samuel was believed to be only eleven when he first heard the voice of God in his life. Eli, who was assigned to grow the prophetic gift in Samuel, gave Samuel instructions and training on how to respond to the voice of God. Like Eli, you too will be used to develop your child's spiritual ear to discern the voice of their heavenly Father. The Bible teaches us that *"My sheep listen to my voice; I know them, and they follow me"* (John 10:27 NLT).

Throughout Scripture, God is metaphorically described as the "Good Shepherd," and His children are likened to sheep. As the result of not growing up on a farm or in an environment where the life of a shepherd is familiar, the meaning of many Scriptures like this, unless studied, are not fully understood. The magnitude of what God is saying in John 10:27 is very profound because it not only has deep spiritual meaning, but natural correlations as well.

Sheep are known not to be the smartest of animals on the farm. If left unattended, many of them will end up being eaten by wolves, falling into a pit, getting caught in a bush, or fighting with one another, just to name a few of their demises. Even in modern-day times, shepherds are known to sleep and stay with their sheep. It is the shepherd's voice that sheep long to hear. It's that voice that they have to know and follow in order to survive. They depend on their shepherd's voice. Hearing it means safety, protection, direction, peace, and provision.

Just like the sheep rely on their shepherd, John 10:27 is saying we are the Good Shepherd's sheep and we must depend on Him. As God's children, we must intimately know and depend on His voice to the point where we will not follow the voice of anyone else. If you find that you don't fit into this scenario, be encouraged to know that nothing else matters at this moment but getting into alignment and position to be able to hear God's voice for your life.

In order to teach this life-saving lesson to your child, it must be a spiritual skill that you yourself have developed as well.

Do You Know God's Voice?

To be led by God, you must know His voice. We are trained to use weapons that are not from the natural or earthly realm. One major weapon is spiritual discernment, which is the ability to understand and perceive a spiritual situation through divine senses. Our ability to discern spiritual activity, good or bad, comes from our ability to discern God. The greater level you can discern God's voice, His character, and His movements, the greater level for you to discern into the spirit realm. Period.

God is spirit; actually He is "The Spirit." His way of communication with you is most likely the same way the enemy tries to communicate and attack you as well. How does God speak? How do you hear His voice? *I believe there is no limit to the ways God can get our attention and communicate,* but a few common ways include: dreams, visions, thoughts, through His Word, through your physical body senses, through prophets, through the everyday such as road signs, movies, circumstances, open and closed doors. If you pay attention, these are probably the same avenues that the enemy likes to use to get messages to you. He may send you a scary dream or a perverted thought, try to entice you to read a dirty book or send demonic burnings of lust to your body, your senses.

When you have identified these demonic tactics, you can counteract the attacks that are being sent your way. It would be easy if we could just pick up a bat and start swinging at them and hit them out of the ballpark; unfortunately, as discussed in previous chapters, you cannot fight a spiritual battle with natural resources. We have to be more strategic than that. It's important for us to gain knowledge of the heavenly plan that will ensure victory over this invisible enemy that wants to wrestle with us.

Since this book is directed toward teaching your little wonder, how do we as adults take everything we have discussed so far and translate it to a child? Very, divinely. Each child is different, and the way they perceive and learn is unique to them. Let your first assignment for this chapter be to ask the Father for the best ways to teach your child how to know His voice. Though ideas and activities will be presented, it's still important to invite the Holy Spirit to be present with you and your child as you learn.

You're Not Alone

Much of what is expected of us as parents can be challenging; and at times you may find yourself wondering, *How is it even possible for me to know all I need to know to raise a godly child?* Be encouraged to know that you are not alone. I believe it is very important to be aware of the fact that you have a first line of defense—the Chief Intercessor who is constantly making intercession for us, Jesus. Jesus's prayers for you and your child are powerful weapons against the enemy.

Along with the prayers of Chief Intercessor Jesus, we too as parents should be interceding on behalf of our children. It is in prayer that you gain heavenly strategies, which come by hearing God's voice, knowing His ways, and living out of His character.

Now that we understand that important life lesson, let's chat a little more about hearing God's voice.

Hindrances to Hearing God's Voice

When you're first learning anything, you may face challenges before accomplishing your goal. Hindrances you may experience while trying to hear God's voice could include: doubt; fear; distractions; other voices; confusion to name a few.

Doubt is the opposite of faith, and it takes faith to take God at His Word and believe He really does desire to speak to you. Doubting that you're good enough to speak to God can be a wall between you and your heavenly Father. The Word instructs us to *"give all your worries and cares to God"* (1 Peter 5:7 NLT). How can we do that if we are doubting we can come into communion with Him? It takes faith to believe God exists, and it will take that same kind of faith to simply believe He's longing to hear from you.

Fear can stop us from ever hearing His voice. Many are afraid to hear God's voice. During a time when the Israelites saw many miracles in the wilderness and they walked through the sea on dry land while Heaven swallowed up their adversaries, yet they still did not want to hear the Voice who led them to freedom. Why? Fear! They pushed for Moses to speak to the God who had thunder in His voice. I am here to tell you that the only thunder you will hear in His voice is His thundering love for you. Do not allow fear to stop you from venturing into the loving voice of your God.

Distractions may actually be the top three hindrances to hearing the voice of God. In today's society, quiet time seems to be a punishment. Electronics have literally taken over a whole generation of children who have not mastered the skill of being still.

Not being able to settle into a place where they can focus on one thing—one very important thing, I might add—God's voice, is a tragedy. As the parent, you may need to set order and help your children prioritize their days. Having them spend devotional time before doing anything else is training them into the mind-set that speaking and spending time with God is the most important part of their day. My first question after saying good morning to my children is, "did you tell God, good morning?"

Other voices and confusion are common hindrances to hearing God's voice. Remember, when God speaks, He never leaves us confused. He comes to set order and separate light from darkness. Many times, though, we hear the voice of God clearly, but then we lose it or can't remember what He said because all we hear are all the other voices speaking to us from social media, the television, our phones, or people we may admire, respect, and look up to. We have to learn to let God's voice be the loudest voice we hear. When He speaks, it's majorly important to guard what was spoken versus minimize it under the voice of people who influence us.

God Hears Everything

Unlike any other God or the enemy, Jehovah is omnipresent. *How can God hear my prayer in the United States and someone else's prayer on the other side of the world?* This supernatural ability is what makes Him God. This superhero trait is called being omnipresent.

He said He will never leave or forsake us; with this revelation, we can assume that God hears and sees everything. As His kids, we do not have to beg to get Him to listen to us. He is forever open and ready to commune with His children. Whenever you're ready, He's right there completely focused on you, all you have to do is lean on into Him.

God Wants to Be Your Best Friend

Approach your heavenly Father as a child. Not with many words to impress, but with a real and authentic desire to hear His voice. God honors our small steps toward Him. He is also a rewarder of those who diligently and consistently seek Him. *Consistency is the key!* It's important to not give up if you don't gain the results you desire the first time. Hearing His voice is a lifelong journey, and I believe we will forever be growing in hearing the voice of God in our lives.

The Father loves to hide things, hold our hands, and give us hints into finding them—because it's not all about the result, it's more about the relationship that is being built in the journey.

It is the glory of God to conceal a matter, but the glory of kings to search out a matter (Proverbs 25:2 NKJV).

It's glorious to be able to journey with the God of Heaven and earth to gain wisdom beyond our age or education, strategies not printed in the halls of universities. Love, peace, joy, prosperity, and victorious living are just some of the benefits of coming into relationship with Him and hearing His voice.

Be encouraged to have the patience to daily discover and find the voice of God in your life. I count it a privilege and an honor to say, "He spoke to me, and I heard His voice." That is the greatest joy of all time. I encourage you to be willing to take a lifelong journey with your heavenly Father to uncover and discover the many ways that He is speaking to you. Do not limit the ways and methods by which He desires to communicate. Be open, be looking, and be aware!

Be willing and open to find God everywhere—in nature, on a street sign, in a movie, as a feeling deep inside, a prophetic voice, through His Word, and so on. Teach your child that God speaks in a variety of ways. "Can you find Him to hear Him?" is a game that translates into a spiritual skill that will make your child a spiritual warrior of warriors. Teaching them that they can go to God for *everything* and know that He will never mock them, expose, or condemn them. This is another piece of powerful information for all believers.

Story Time

I can't end a chapter without a story. So...training our children to hear the voice of God has a reciprocal blessing. I can never forget the time when my son shared with me a dream he had. He knew that this particular dream was a "God dream." Not only was it a God-given dream, but it was a dream of warning and confirmation all at the same time. I hugged and thanked him for being obedient to God's voice and sharing the dream.

As a parent, you have to be humble enough to say, "God will even speak to me through my child." A lack of humility will cause us to miss crucial messages. I said it earlier, "There is no small Holy Spirit." Training your child to "hear" can start as soon as they are able to effectively communicate. There is no limit to what God can do through them when they can clearly hear God's voice for themselves. Then they are fully armed and dangerous to the kingdom of darkness and a major asset in your home and life. Be open to hear and listen!

Now that you have a framework, the following are some summary points to share with your child. It's important to have your children know that God is not a scary voice ready to tell them how bad they are. He is the Good Shepherd longing to chat with them about how great they are. Now let's get them excited to embark on a life-changing adventure of learning the voice of their God.

Points to Ponder

- God longs to speak with you.
- He doesn't want to scare or condemn you
- Kids can hear God too
- You can tell him EVERYTHING.
- Doubt, fear, distractions, and other voices can hinder you hearing God's voice clearly.
- God's voice is the most important voice you will ever hear.
- Learning to hear His voice may take time, and that's OK.

Remember that...

- God's voice will not tell you to do bad things.
- His voice will sound just like His words in the Bible.

- His voice is loving and kind.
- His voice brings peace.
- His voice reveals wisdom.
- His voice is hard to ignore and forget.
- His voice brings wholeness deep inside you.

"Hello, God, It's Me" Activity

Practice listening for God's voice. When we listen correctly, it yields results. It's also important to practice speaking to God through prayer with your children. Teach them that prayer is a conversation, it's speaking and then listening. The listening part is the most crucial. Let them know it takes time and to constantly be open to how God decides to speak to them.

The following is a template you can use to assist your children if they are a little nervous about starting off a conversation with God.

Let's practice praying to God. It's easy. You can start by saying, "Hello, God, it's me!" Now you try it.

Hello, God, it's me _____
(insert child's name). *Thank You for always listening to me and wanting to hear what I have to say. Today, I* _____ *(fill in the blank). Something really cool that happened today was* _____ *(fill in the blank). Something that made me sad today was* _____ *(fill in the blank).*

Parent: The following are some follow-up questions. Once asked, try sitting quietly for about three minutes and listen for an answer.

_____ *(say child's name), don't feel rejected or upset if you feel you did not hear anything back from God. Remember, He heard you because He's omnipresent, that means He's everywhere. And He's omniscient, which means He knows everything.*

_____ *(child's name), another way to pray with God is to ask Him for His advice. You can say, "Hi, Father God. What do You think I should do about* _____?" *Or, "Hi, Father God, do You have any advice on how I can deal with this situation?" Or, "Hi, Father God, what do You really think about me?"*

OK, _____ *(child's name), let's just sit for a while and focus on what God wants to tell you. Let's think about Jesus and how much He loves you and how much He wants to be part of your life.*

Chapter Seven

THE WORD IS A WEAPON

Speaking the Word of God Is a Weapon

The Word of God is the standard by which all our ways, thoughts, actions, deeds, and motives should be measured against. Our concept of morality should be defined by the Word of God, not by culture, and not by what we as individuals desire or believe to be right in our own eyes. The Word of God is the mind of God. It intricately displays the character and the love of God for His children. It has the power to give life, it can be used for correction, definition of life, strategy for the journey and instructions on how to live life to our fullest potentials.

> *I have hidden your word in my heart, that I might not sin against you* (Psalm 119:11 NIV).

To hide God's Word in our hearts is to have it become imprinted on the DNA of our being. It's about knowing the Word, understanding the Word, and obeying the Word. The psalmist understood that in order to not sin against God, we have to fully understand what God considers sinful and inappropriate behavior against His ways.

We also should fully grasp the concept that it's not enough to just know it, we have to bury it deep down within us until it becomes the place from where we respond from.

The Bible does not leave us without an example on how to use the word against the enemy when he comes to challenge the God in us. Let's take a look:

The Temptation of Jesus

Then Jesus was led by the Spirit into the wilderness to be tempted there by the devil. For forty days and forty nights he fasted and became very hungry. During that time the devil came and said to him, "If you are the Son of God, tell these stones to become loaves of bread."

*But Jesus told him, "No! **The Scriptures say,** 'People do not live by bread alone, but by every word that comes from the mouth of God.'"*

Then the devil took him to the holy city, Jerusalem, to the highest point of the Temple, and said, "If you are the Son of God, jump off! For the Scriptures say, 'He will order his angels to protect you. And they will hold you up with their hands so you won't even hurt your foot on a stone.'"

*Jesus responded, "**The Scriptures also say,** 'You must not test the Lord your God.'"*

Next the devil took him to the peak of a very high mountain and showed him all the kingdoms of the world and their glory. "I will give it all to you," he said, "if you will kneel down and worship me."

*"Get out of here, Satan," Jesus told him. "For **the Scriptures say,** 'You must worship the Lord your God and serve only him'"* (Matthew 4:1-10 NLT).

Jesus not only knew the Word, He fully and skillfully was able to use it against any and every accusation thrown at him by the enemy. The interesting thing about this text is that the enemy knew the Word as well. He actually thought that he could use it to trip up the Son of God, causing Him to abort His assignment.

The enemy's tactics have not changed over time; from Adam and Eve until today he will attempt to twist the Words of God to lure us into lifestyles that are enmity toward God. That's why it is so important not only to *read* God's Word but to *study it* as well. In the armor of God, the Word is likened to a sword. It is the only piece of armor that is offensive in nature versus defensive.

Your Word above Your Name

I will worship toward Your holy temple, and praise Your name for Your lovingkindness and Your truth; for You have magnified Your word above all Your name (Psalm 138:2 NKJV).

The Father regards His Word above His very name. With that understanding, we must value His Word and understand how powerful it really is. In homes worldwide, a go-to weapon against the many spiritual battles believers face is simply declaring the name of Jesus. I agree there is much power in the name of Jesus, but a major biblical example many believers miss when combatting the attacks of the enemy is to declare and live what is written in God's

Word. The Father's words can never fail or return to Him void or unaccomplished.

> *So shall My word be that goes forth from My mouth;*
> *it shall not return to Me void, but it shall accomplish*
> *what I please, and it shall prosper in the thing which I*
> *sent it* (Isaiah 55:11 NKJV).

Spoken words never die, they are forever either creating or destroying. That's why the Bible encourages us to watch what we say because there is life and death in the power of our tongues (Proverbs 18:21). The good news is that words spoken by our Abba Father are forever alive, breathing, building, and working on our behalf. The Word of God is our most powerful resource that truly has the ability to extinguish the fiery darts of the evil one.

We Are the Kingdom

There are military and Kingdom terminology throughout the whole Bible. Words like "citizen, laws, king, armor," and so on. I believe there are some hidden meanings that we can learn from to further assist us with better understanding how to operate in the Kingdom of God. For example, knowing your rights according to the law is a crucial component of being able to make sure all that is owed is appropriated to you. When purchasing equipment or buying a service, many people do not read the terms and conditions, but this can prove to be a huge mistake if there ever was a need for litigation. Many large corporations add clauses to the terms and conditions to ensure a verdict in their favor.

To win a court case, the attorney must not only know the law and statutes, but be able to intricately understand how those laws connect to their client's case to render a verdict in their favor. You may not be a lawyer, but let's just say that your child needed a spiritual one and the Bible contained the statutes—terms and conditions—that would need to be understood to render a verdict in your child's favor of "not depressed," "chains broken," or "mind free from torment." Would you find it necessary now to know what the Word of God says?

As a citizen of the Kingdom, it is imperative that you fully understand the terms and conditions to successfully live in the Kingdom of God, especially the terms that not only connect to your natural life but also your eternal soul. In the Word of God are hidden clauses that are Spirit-revealed to ensure that you and your child live a complete life of victory.

Knowing God's Promises Is a Weapon

Anytime our lives do not reflect what Christ died for, we have the right to get upset and become frustrated enough to seek Heaven for change. Many are living below God's standards and level of living because they do not know what the Word says about how they should and could live. Knowing and understanding the promises of God is a weapon. Do you know that there was an inheritance left to you and your child? The promises released in the Word of God are the details of that inheritance.

Let's take a look a just a few of God's promises revealed in the Bible:

- Exodus 14:14 NIV: *"The Lord will fight for you; you need only to be still."*
- Isaiah 40:29 NIV: *"He gives strength to the weary and increases the power of the weak."*
- Isaiah 40:31 NIV: *"But those who trust in the Lord will find new strength. They will soar high on wings like eagles; they will run and not grow weary, they will walk and not be faint."*
- Mark 11:24 NLT: *"I tell you, you can pray for anything, and if you believe that you've received it, it will be yours."*
- Psalm 23:4 NLT: *"Even when I walk through the darkest valley, I will not be afraid, for you are close beside me. Your rod and your staff protect and comfort me."*

The Bible houses the greatest stories ever to be told!

Reading the Word Is a Weapon

Nowadays reading the Bible is not the top thing on this generation's "cool things to do" list. With so many competing priorities and fun activities, reading the Bible ranks some place between going to the dentist and New Year's resolutions. I have to admit that not all the time I read am I jumping for joy; but what I have come to understand is, like exercising, taking medicine, or eating our vegetables, it's necessary and can save mine or my child's life. That revelation alone causes me to have a greater level of priority.

The Word Is Prophetic

What challenge am I going to face today that this morning's Scripture will help me conquer? What virtue did I read about last night that will keep me from getting fired? What persons in the Bible will I need to learn about to see how they stood in troubling times? Reading the Bible can be described to our children more as an adventure versus something God is mandating. Be encouraged to present the Bible as a book that has encrypted hidden mysteries yet to be revealed. Challenge them to search it out for problem-solving Scriptures that will help when handling everyday issues.

There is not one problem they are facing today that the Word of God does not address in some kind of way. The question is when they are of age, can they seek and find it? Noah was ridiculed for obeying God; Moses dealt with feeling incompetent; Jeremiah faced mean, stubborn bullies; David dealt with rejection and faced giants; Solomon was rich but questioned the purpose of life; Sarah had to trust God even in her old age; Ruth lost everything but still remained faithful; Daniel was persecuted for not adapting to the culture of the day; on and on you can find examples in the Bible of how our ancestors in faith overcame every situation that we and our children must too fight to overcome.

The Greatest Stories Ever Told

I remember reading to my children when they were very young, sharing some of the greatest stories ever told right out of the Word of God. They loved it. There were many times when they would say, "Just one more story...please?" My son tells me that a lot of the stories that he knows today were from those times when I read to him when he was just a child. I didn't realize that reading to him out of the Word of God was forging a love and desire to know more, to seek God for himself. It was also providing a discipline and a desire to read for himself once he got older.

There is something supernatural about the Word of God. You can read one Scripture one week and it speaks to a broken place in you. And you can read the same Scripture the week after and get something completely different out of it. Reading and studying the Bible is a necessary and crucial spiritual discipline to train in your child. When they are young, encouraging the reading of God's Word as a daily ritual helps them not stray away from it when they are older.

I remember for me growing up, reading the Bible was hard because I really just did not understand it. Today, though, there are many more translations that make God's Word easier to understand. There are children's Bibles, teen Bibles, new beginner Bibles, worship Bibles, 365 daily Bibles, and The Message Bible is translated into regular, everyday language. I honestly feel that there really is no excuse any more not to find a Bible that speaks to where you are in your individual journey. Investing in an age-appropriate Bible is teaching your child you care—it's important that they have one they can read and understand.

Hearing the Word Is a Weapon

Throughout the Bible, from the Old Testament to the New Testament, the Bible repeats key themes connecting to hearing the Word of God like, *"Hear ye, the word of the Lord."* (Jeremiah 2:4) And, *"Give ear to the teachings oh you Israel."* (Psalm 78:1) On and on I found these alarm-style requests to God's people being repeated throughout Scripture.

One thing about our Father is that He does not waste words or repeat because He doesn't have anything else to say. God is such a loving Father that He never wants to be accused of not providing His children every tool necessary to win. Knowing now that throughout Scripture God wants us to hear the word over and over, the only next question to ask is, why?

Two Scriptures that first come to mind to support the need for hearing the Word of God are the following:

So faith comes from hearing [what is told], and what is heard comes by the [preaching of the] message concerning Christ (Romans 10:17 Amplified Bible).

And it is impossible to please God without faith. Anyone who wants to come to him must believe that God exists and that he rewards those who sincerely seek him (Hebrews 11:6 NLT).

If faith is the very thing that is required for us to please God, why would He not constantly remind us of the importance of the very thing that helps build it? Hearing something over and over and over gets deep down into your mind, then into your heart, then into your emotions—and ultimately to the core of who you are. God wants His Word to be like the song that you just can't get out of your head.

Worship Music Goes a Long Way

During the seasons when we were experiencing extremely bad attacks, some of our go-to tactics were to saturate the atmosphere with worship music. Not just the songs from a Christian doo-wop band, I'm talking about music with the Word of God as the lyrics. Some of my greatest encounters and dreams come when I fall asleep to anointed worship music or listening to the Word of God on the Mp3 player. This is a great idea for your children as well. Play Word-of-God music while they are asleep. Do not under-estimate the power of how deeply it goes and the impact it has on them.

YOU CANNOT REGURGITATE WHAT YOU NEVER DIGESTED.

Memorizing the Word Is a Weapon

A definition of "memorize" is commit to memory or *learn by heart*. I really like this way of defining the word, as it connects to the importance of memorizing the Word of God. To learn by heart is so important. When I think of that, I am reminded of the times when I spoke from the heart, or when I taught from the heart. Many say the most powerful speeches are the ones less scripted and spoken more *"from the heart."* In the context of what I'm trying to get you the parent to grasp, is that in order to speak from the heart, there has to be something written on it. If you're going to write something, why not let it be the Word of God? Teaching your child to memorize Scripture is a weapon like no other.

Yay! Story Time

Moriah came home from school one day and ran over to me so excited to share about her day. I asked her several questions to provoke more details. I don't remember which question, but one of them reminded her of a situation that happened earlier that day.

She began to share about how a little boy in her class called her ugly. So I asked her, "How did that make you feel?"

She said, "Mad."

"OK, that's a normal reaction. How did you respond?"

"Well, I told him, 'No I'm not, I am fearfully and beautifully made.'"

I just smiled at her and said, "You know what? You're right. The only truth you have to believe is what God says about you."

She smiled so widely, gave me a hug, and ran off to play with her siblings. What could have been the outcome if Moriah was not empowered to memorize Scripture or she was not affirmed in who she was? She would not have had any truth written on her heart to pull from. The enemy desires to write something on their hearts or even overwrite on what's there. That's why it's so important to memorize Scripture—including songs with lyrics that cite Scripture.

*"Keep my commands and live, And my law as the apple of your eye. Bind them on your fingers; **Write them on the tablet of your heart"** (Proverbs 2:3-4).*

What makes me sad is that many children are fed lies that they can't refute because their hearts are empty of God's truths about them. I pray that your child will not be placed in that category. Memorizing Scripture does not have to be an arduous task. It's something that the whole family can do together. My suggestion is to make it fun, place on the refrigerator or centralized place, and possibly add incentives especially for your younger children. God rewards us for our righteous deeds, so why can't we do the same for our kids? We can!

Points to Ponder

- Declaring the Word is a weapon.
- The Bible is a prescription for all of our life problems.
- The Bible can be a fun adventure to journey through.
- Reading and studying the Bible is a weapon.
- Knowing and declaring what's written in God's Word is a weapon against attacks.
- Hearing the Word is a weapon that builds great faith.
- Memorizing the Word is a weapon.

Prayer Declaration

Heavenly Father, in the name of Jesus, I thank You for not leaving us without instructions on how to live a prosperous life. Give me and _____ (insert child's name) *a deeper love for Your Word. Open our eyes to truly see Your heart's intentions. Let Your Word be a lamp for our feet to see where we are going and a light on our path. Light up any darkness in our lives by the truth of Your Word. Continue to show us how You see us, and thank You for revealing through Your Word whatever You need us to know in this season. In Your Son's name we pray, amen.*

Speak Life

Speaking affirmations is healthy. There is power in speaking the Word of God over our lives. Scriptures teach us that our faith is increased the more we hear the Word of God. Speaking daily affirmations is a strategic way to speak life until you and your child feel alive in Christ. The following is a sample affirmation; and this chapter's activation is going to be for you and your child to write your own affirmation using the Word of God. The goal is to commit the affirmation to memory and build a healthy habit of declaring it every morning.

Affirmation example:

I am a child of the Most High God, and I am fearfully and wonderfully made. I am so special to God that He knows how many hairs I have on my head, and every tear I cry He keeps in a bottle. I was created for purpose and bought with a price. When I am weak, Lord, You are my strength. No weapon formed against me will prosper. For God so loved me that He gave His only Son for me; because I believe on Him, I will have everlasting life.

OK, now it's your and your child's turn. Write away!

Chapter Eight

BREAKING GENERATIONAL CYCLES, EARLY

Breaking Chords Meant to Strangle

Generational curses are real, and if not broken will feel empowered to keep hopping from generation to generation. This chapter provides the fundamental understanding of generational curses and how they can and need to be broken in your life and your child's life.

Breaking covenant with a father's or mother's unhealthy ways is a weapon. Deciding to break covenant with every lie, thought, or action that wars against the knowledge of who God says your child is called to be, is not only a weapon but a strategy to weaken the enemy's permission to remain. James 4:7 (NIV) states, *"Resist the devil, and he will flee from you."* Resisting and breaking covenant with ungodly principles from the past empowers you to live a life of sustained freedom.

Every curse sent to desecrate us was nailed and murdered at the Cross; but if resuscitation is performed on that curse by the power of agreement, that curse has a right to perform. Let's expose the enemy's entry points and make ourselves aware of how to uproot it once and for all.

Breaking Cycles

If allowed, sin (thoughts and actions that are opposite to God's) can travel from one generation to the next creating vicious cycles that need to be broken. They cannot just be ignored; someone within that generation needs to do the hard work of murdering the cycle and uprooting it so that it is no longer permitted to perform in the next generation.

There are two different viewpoints on generational curses. Some believe that curses and the guilt are no longer passed down from the father to the son, based on several Scriptures that address curses. I do believe a portion of this idea because the Scripture teaches us that Jesus became a curse/sin so that we can be redeemed from the curse of the law. On the Cross any and everything vile and sinful imaginable act was placed on Him; and when He died and arose again on the third day, what was appropriated for us was an opportunity to overcome through Christ anything that He defeated on that Cross. Just like sicknesses, sin showing up in our lives is permitted—if we allow it.

In other words, I'll never forget hearing the answer of one of my mentors when I asked, "What's your thoughts on, if a Christian can have a demon?" His answer was simple, "Christians can have whatever they want to have." The key is this, if we don't want to have a generational curse, we don't have to have it. Jesus beat whatever we are struggling with, and through His sacrifice, we can beat it too.

There is a family I know personally who for three generations straight the women all birthed their firstborn children out of wedlock at the exact age of sixteen. Another family, for four generations straight, all the men abused and beat their wives. Another family, several generations deep of women all lived on the welfare system. I can go on and on with stories of generation after generation having the same struggles, same sins, same demons. Those situations are *not* coincidental. Those are spiritual mind-sets, behaviors, and strongholds that need to be uprooted out of the family bloodline.

I'll never forget the time when my husband received a prophetic word that he would be a generation curse breaker in his family. A snippet of his story is that his father was in and out of jail his whole life and introduced the family to a life of physical abuse. His father was addicted to drugs and had many struggles that ultimately ended his life at the early age of thirty-seven.

For many years my husband was so afraid that he would not live past the age of his father; but now being forty-four he has already broken the assignment of early death and a life of being in and out of prison. My husband is named after his uncle who died from meningitis before he was sixteen years old. At the age of sixteen, my husband was diagnosed with meningitis that hospitalized him for over two weeks. This same sickness was on assignment to perpetuate a generational early death—but because of God's grace, he survived!

We Have to Choose

Jesus took the verdict of guilty upon Himself. But like salvation, we still must choose to allow the work, benefits, and results to be performed in our lives by breaking the cycles and choosing not to perpetuate the same behaviors. During Old Covenant times, if the father sinned, the whole house paid many times with their lives. The New Covenant says grace can come in to save not just the children but the father as well—if he chooses to repent. Curses, also known as behaviors and ways of thinking, can be broken by the next generation choosing to repent, which simply put means to change the way you think.

As mentioned in Chapter Two there was a time early on in my parenting journey when I noticed that my two older kids were being plagued with fear. They were fearful to do almost anything. I remember speaking with my mother about this because it was very concerning. I too was on my own personal journey of breaking fear out of my life, and to see it bubbling up in my kids was so heartbreaking.

After sharing this with my mom, she shared with me her journey. She told story after story of when she was a child and how she was literally afraid of everything. She missed a lot of opportunities simply because she was afraid. Here in this one conversation, we identified three generations plagued and stifled by the spirit of fear. This is where my "power up" moment came into place because I did not want to have the same conversation with my kids when they get older, discussing how fear continued to show up in their kids, my grandkids. I could not stomach the thought of that. Like me, you have to be determined and say, "The buck stops here, no more."

How Hard Can it Be?

I am well aware that breaking cycles for some may not be as simple as they want it to be. The reality is that anything that has roots generations long, Heaven's assistance will be necessary. I wasn't looking for "easy" necessarily, what kept and continues to keep me focused is the mental image I have of removing the spirit of fear off of life support with a "do not resuscitate" order in place. I have a saying that I use pretty frequently, "God reveals to either, heal or murder something out of our lives."

Reading this book is an indication that there are some things in your life and your child's life that Heaven may be saying, "We have had enough." Since the Father wills in us to do of His good pleasure, the very exposure of what's hidden says that its time. There is no cookie cutter template answer of how hard it's going to be; but if you're ready to move forward, there is grace available through Christ to claim victory over what's trying to beat up you and your family.

A Painful Journey

I'm pretty sure my journey was very painful for others to watch. I am a natural-born introvert forced into an extrovert's world. I was haunted by the unspoken voices of people, filled with anxiety that people were watching me; I had fears of failing, being successful, messing up, being a total disappointment, never making it, not being a good wife, not being a good parent, not accomplishing my dreams—on and on I can add to the list of fears that simply overshadowed my life. Since this spirit was generational, it was allowed in my life and sometimes it screamed. You may wonder, *Well, how did you break it?*

I believe that people are assigned to our lives for many different reasons and there are times when God will send you places that will challenge the fear right out of you. That was exactly my case.

The first time is when I was asked by our former pastor to open the service with prayer. I think I almost wet my pants, like literally. I begged him to choose someone else, pleaded and pleaded to let me off the hook, but to no avail, the request did not change. It wasn't that I didn't want to do it, I was just simply too afraid.

When the microphone was handed to me, it was visibly shaking in my hand because I was so afraid. I prayed silently, *God, I can't do this without You. If You don't stand up in me, this is going to be embarrassing for You and me.* Well, I got through it only because I leaned in and on the Father that never fails you in your time of need. Little did I know that was Day One of breaking generational curses class 101. Till this day, whenever I'm presented with a chance, I refuse to give in to fear, therefore breaking it— one opportunity at a time.

Anytime you are presented an opportunity where you normally would respond from the old harmful family mind-set, chose the better way of thinking—and lean on God.

Self-Awareness

When it comes to your children, they may not know how to conceptualize the terms "generational curses or cycles," but they may understand "bad behaviors" or "unhealthy ways." The first step in helping your child break what appears to be a potential generational cycle in their lives is to first make them aware of it.

A Key to Breaking Cycles is Self-awareness

A mother sat down with her son and had to have a very hard conversation. It broke her heart to do so, but she saw her son beginning to display unhealthy behaviors that mirrored that of his father. Behaviors of lying, manipulating women, and so on. It hurt to see this, and she knew that if these behaviors would go unchecked, he too could find himself in a cycle of using women rather than respecting them. No one wants to find this kind of cycle breeding in the heart of their child, but too often it may go ignored or explained away, and the necessary steps of awareness and uprooting never takes place. When confronting the issues, there is also the challenging balancing act of not exposing the other parent to save face and not cause reputational hazards.

The conversation was presented gently by the mother with examples of facts versus perception and emotion. Though eye-opening for the son, he too saw some of his behaviors that were not healthy, and he desired to change. As a result of the conversation, the mother was able to gracefully challenge and expose any behavior that mirrored what was discussed in the conversation. The son was given tools to learn how to be self-aware; and when presented with opportunities to walk in unhealthy behaviors, he now realizes that he has authority over what was trying to perform in his life. He now has tools of engagement, is made aware of what is possible, and takes on the challenge of breaking a generational cycle that the previous generation did not or could not break.

Real and Hard Conversations

These conversations are real and sometimes real hard. My parents conceived all of their children including myself and four other siblings, while married. The irony of my story is that all four of my sisters and brothers, including myself, conceived our firstborn children unwed. We were not raised this way nor were we exposed to a world where this was encouraged or prevalent.

Wow, all five? Where did this come from?

I honestly don't have an answer for that in this book, maybe in a follow-up one. But what I do know is that now we have the responsibility in making sure this behavior does not matriculate down through our bloodline to our children. All five of us have our own story and I dare not attempt to tell theirs, but what I can say is when I very young I experienced a lot of trauma and rejection that propelled my journey down a very rebellious, dark road. When my eldest two children were old enough, I shared this journey with them. I shared the why behind it all. What made me make the decisions that I did and the ins and outs of my brokenness that caused me to make unhealthy choices. It's not fluffy, but it's real.

I felt led to be open and transparent. I shared my struggles of being a single parent and the road to getting healing from the distorted opinions that I had about myself. They appreciated this conversation and reference it quite often during times when they were battling with something that was likened to a dark place in me. My vulnerability and openness flung wide the doors of dialog and journeying with my kids so that they now know that they do not have to be ashamed of hidden struggles that more than likely were passed down to them by their mother. Now, we can break it together.

My story by no means is a guaranteed template on how to break unhealthy family cycles, but displaying authenticity is the heart of our God and can be a formidable tool to use. My hope is that while sharing my story, you can find peace in knowing that real conversations, openness, and awareness can be tools used to expose and uproot the plans of the enemy. Your tools may look different from mine, that's OK as long as the end result is the dismantling of ugly ways attempting to be perpetuated down to your child.

Auditing and Measuring

Not knowing what unhealthy cycles need to be broken in your child is the enemy to breaking them. It is important for you as a parent to begin auditing your child's behaviors. Are there certain ways of thinking that you can identify as first, unhealthy, and second, contrary to how the Father would desire the child to operate in the Kingdom of God? This may be challenging for some; because in order to identify what's unhealthy in your child, you will need to also face what's unhealthy in you.

The measuring stick we need to use is the Kingdom of God. The Kingdom of God is righteousness or God's ways peace, and joy. Any action that does not bear the fruit of the Kingdom can be placed on the audit report; then once reviewed, you can determine if it fits into the generational cycle or the new cycle bucket. Through using the Word of God, talk with your child about why these behaviors are unhealthy and could pose serious consequences in their future. Second, share with them the steps of self-awareness and how to red flag thoughts and behaviors that need to be broken in their lives. This exercise could be one of the most important lessons your child could learn to thrust them into the all of who God has called them to be.

Points to Ponder

- Generational behaviors are real, and unhealthy ones need to be broken.
- The guilt has been removed from the next generation, but changing the way you think is crucial.
- You break the cycles one cycle at a time.
- You may need to have a hard conversation with your child, it's OK.
- Authenticity is a door to breakthrough.
- It's important to routinely audit your child's life for unhealthy cycles, mind-sets, behaviors.

Prayer Declaration

Father God, I thank You that You want to see me and _____ (insert child's name) *become free from the cycles that have plagued our family for generations. I ask that Your Holy Spirit will expose what needs to be removed and uprooted out of our lives. Highlight mind-sets that do not mirrors Yours. Give me the strategies to walk* _____ (insert child's name) *through the journey to complete wholeness. In Your Son's name I pray, amen.*

It's Audit Time

Let's conduct an audit. Write down any behaviors, beliefs, ways, or cycles that you are trusting the Father to help you break in your life or in the life of your child:

Chapter Nine

PUNISHMENT VERSUS DISCIPLINE

"Is This Going To Hurt?"

Discipline is a weapon against the enemy of God's children. This chapter introduces a possible new concept for you to consider—the importance of partnering with the Holy Spirit about how to discipline and train your child according to each circumstance. Also learning how important it is to partner with the Holy Spirit's all-knowing mind to extract what is really needed to restore, adjust, and correct in our children while using the golden nuggets straight out of Heaven's child-rearing Guidebook—the Bible.

I believe it's imperative to know and understand all possible vehicles of discipline needed to be effective in the numerous stages of your child's life. I will challenge cookie-cutter approaches and generationally passed down ways to punish your children that could be void of love and fueled by frustration and aggravation. We will further explore the idea that discipline absent from the strong understanding and feelings of love by a child will be perceived as abuse.

When You Have Kids, You Have Disciples

"Discipline" comes from the Latin word *discipulus, broken down to mean* pupil. While looking at this word we notice "disciple" is neatly tucked within its confines. I love this explanation because it changes how we as parents look at raising our children. If we see them more as disciples versus little people we need to "keep in line," our handling of them and parental approach completely changes.

Most parents would agree that discipline is necessary, but the what, how, when, where, and why are the very things that become grey at times. No "good" parent desires to break their children or emotionally scar them for life; but the reality is, that's what happens when we leave the Holy Spirit out of our child-rearing journey.

This may be a new concept, so let me explain what I mean by inviting the Holy Spirit into child-rearing—by telling you yet another story.

Strong-Willed Kids Rock!

Moriah, my youngest child, is one of the most strong-willed, fun-loving, justice-oriented kids I have ever met. Even from a toddler she knew what she wanted and was OK with running you over to get it. I'll never forget the time she kept touching the electrical socket and my husband went over to her and tapped her hand, saying very sternly, "No, do not touch." Well, Moriah must have felt like that action was unjustified because at two years of age, she walked over to him after he sat down and smacked him back on his hand.

She is described as simply being "fearless." When Moriah was around three years old, getting her to go to bed was the war of wills. My husband and I had a nighttime ritual with all of our kids: announce its time to go to bed, pray over them, tuck them in, turn out the light, and proceed to our own room. Three out of the four kids would adhere to this practice almost perfectly, all but our little Moriah. Right around the age of three, night after night she would revolt by falling out screaming for long periods of time, running in the halls, and just completely go bonkers.

"LOVE IS THE MOST POWERFUL TOOL ON EARTH."
—GOD

At this point, I was not only feeling tested but extremely exhausted and frustrated, because at the time the counsel I kept receiving was, "It's a test of who's going to win, so just be stern, put her back in her bed no matter how many times, and eventually she will give in." One night it was nine times!

After weeks of this charade, it became clear that either something was wrong with her, which it wasn't, or as her parents we were doing something majorly wrong. I remember out of frustration praying and asking the Father, "What is going on with her?

Why is she so rebellious?" That night I went to sleep and I actually had a dream that Moriah was being exasperated and tormented by something, but I didn't know what. I remember that she was so upset and she kept reaching out for me.

I woke up with such empathy and almost sadness rather than frustration for her. The feeling that the dream left in my heart remained the full day. I asked the Father how He wanted me to handle Moriah's nightly tantrums, and instead of Him saying, "Spank her," He spoke these simple but power words, "Love is the most powerful tool on earth." Now that I had the strategy, I was ready for whatever Moriah was about to bring that night.

Needless to say, as soon as we began our nightly ritual with the kids, like clockwork Moriah began hers—but this night's outcome was different. Instead of getting frustrated and harshly communicating to her, I dropped down on the floor with her, grabbed her up in my arms and began affirming her. I spoke over her how special she was to me, how much I loved her, how God's peace will cover her, and how uniquely created she was.

Not even five minutes later, her little body went limp in my arms and her eyes closed shut. I saw such a peace come over her that lasted all night. The next time I saw her was the next morning. The prescription for that particular event was not time out, spankings, or stern conversations. Something within her needed the affirmative love of her mother.

Looking back at that time, I remember that I was gone from the home a lot due to my work schedule. Children many times do not yet have the maturity or aptitude to explain their deepest needs. Heck, it may be even a mystery to them why they act the way they do. But that's OK because the Holy Spirit knows the heart and motives of His children and is the revealer of all truth. If we take the time to ask Him, we will get the answers we need, but were seeking elsewhere in vain. From that night on, I began to consistently invite the Holy Spirit into my disciplinary journey with my kids.

> But when the Father sends the Advocate as my repre-sentative—that is, **the Holy Spirit**—he **will teach you everything** and will **remind you** of everything I have told you (John 14:26 NLT).

Are You Committed?

You have to know that this way of discipline takes time, much patience, and consistency. You have to agree to rip up the template responses that were probably handed down to you from your parents or caregiver. Every outbreak and rebellious response is an opportunity to ask, "Holy Spirit, what are we doing here?"

I encourage you to sign here if you agree to be committed to disciplining according to the Holy Spirit's guidance:

_____

(Parent Signature)

Most parents, especially first-time parents, are afraid of making mistakes, doing something wrong, and not becoming that perfect parent they think they should be. I assume this desire is connected to the theory that perfect parents create perfect kids. First, let me help you with a bit of reality—you *will* make mistakes, you *will* do it wrong, and you *will* never be a perfect parent because you, we, are human and not even close to perfect. Even if you could come

0.01 millimeters close to perfection, that still is not a guarantee that your kids will be perfect.

How do I know this? Very simply, our Father God was the most perfect, loving Father to Adam and Eve and to His Israelite children, yet history reveals that even with a perfect Father rebellion is common. Humans are born and shaped in iniquity; rebellion, foolishness, is stored up in the heart of a child (Proverbs 22:15 NKJV). Everyone, even our kids need to go through a process, circumcision of the heart, training, and discipline in order to bloom into their most whole place.

When we fail to provide consequences in the lives of our children as a result of their rebellious actions, we paint a tainted picture of an unrealistic world. We are also setting them up to have a very frustrated existence and a head-on collision with a disgruntled and rude awakening. The challenge parents face is that if they do not discipline their children, the world and the world's systems will. An example of a world system having to step in and correct behavior is the criminal justice system—serious consequences from actions that have gone "unchecked" at home.

Children actually need to be taught how to receive discipline, correction, and feedback. I find in my current profession as a training supervisor that so many from the next generation have not been taught how to receive and apply feedback. It seems as if their parents told them daily their whole lives just how wonderful they were; so when true feedback comes, they fall apart and act like the world is crashing in on them. I've never seen anything like it.

Coming to this realization, I very quickly began to teach my children that feedback is healthy. I stress that to them that discipline and learning what parents, teachers, and later bosses, expect doesn't mean they are failures and are worthless. Constructive feedback and appropriate discipline can be opportunities for them to self-reflect and find any areas that could be improved to add beauty to who they are.

Constantly hearing how great they are and never receiving areas of improvement is a delusional way for children to live. Soon, very soon, they will run into someone who doesn't think they're as cute as their parents do. My advice is to teach your children how to solicit feedback, which keeps them in the driver's seat of their maturing journey.

What, When, Where, Why, and How

Chastisement (noun: a rebuke or strong reprimand) is love and a weapon against an unruly heart.

Hebrews 12:6 (English Standard Version) says, *"The Lord disciplines the one he loves, and chastises every son whom he receives."*

The Message Bible says it this way:

> *So don't feel sorry for yourselves. Or have you forgotten how good parents treat children, and that God regards you as his children? My dear child, don't shrug off God's discipline, but don't be crushed by it either. It's the child he loves that he disciplines; the child he embraces, he also corrects. God is educating you; that's why you must never drop out. He's treating you as dear children.*
>
> *This trouble you're in isn't punishment; it's training, the normal experience of children. Only irresponsible parents leave children to fend for themselves. Would*

you prefer an irresponsible God? We respect our own parents for training and not spoiling us, so why not embrace God's training so we can truly live?

While we were children, our parents did what seemed best to them. But God is doing what is best for us, training us to live God's holy best. At the time, discipline isn't much fun. It always feels like it's going against the grain. Later, of course, it pays off handsomely, for it's the well-trained who find themselves mature in their relationship with God (Hebrews 12:5-11).

I believe that nine out of ten parents would agree their children do need discipline; but the challenge is when, where, why, and how? Before I attempt to provide my answers to some of those open-ended questions, let's lay another foundational understanding of the importance of discipline.

I want to first present the idea that discipline is *a* weapon to assist in stifling the growth of a rebellious heart that would ultimately lead to destruction. Webster's dictionary describes discipline as "control gained by enforcing obedience or order; orderly prescribed conduct or pattern of behavior; training that corrects, molds, or perfects the mental faculties or moral character." Scriptures instruct parents to *"Train up a child in the way he should go, and when he is old he will not depart from it* [those teachings]" (Proverbs 22:6 NKJV). The Word also instructs parents: *"Whoever spares the rod hates their children, but the one who loves their children is careful to discipline them"* (Proverbs 13:24 NIV), which we will fully dissect later in this chapter.

170

Discipline can either be the response to a disobedient action or at the same time be the reason why disobedience wasn't someone's response. Let me say it like this, when you see children behaving well, very respectful, not unruly, you may think to yourself, *Wow, they are very disciplined.* What you are really thinking is, *Even though these kids were presented with several opportunities to "cut up," because of their mental and physical resolve, they resisted the urge to do so.* I want to present to you that children are *not* born orderly, obedient, and trained. Children are cultivated into those behaviors. In essence, they are *trained* that way.

I know many people do not like the term "train" because it's used in connection with animals; but training is not a dirty word, it's what loving parents should be doing, training up their children in the way they should be going or responding. At some point in those well-behaved children's lives their parents talked to them, and talked to them, and talked to them AND... talked to them. Lol, OK, you get the point. I'm pretty sure that there were other forms of correction or other consequences to let those kids know that when they didn't follow direction, their disobedience would cause uncomfortable or unwanted results.

Let's Chat

Let's chat about that controversial *rod!* Like I used to, many believers are quick to defend the rearing of children by using corporal punishment by quoting Scriptures without doing a deep dive into what's really trying to be communicated.

But Psalm 23:4 states, *"Your rod and Your staff, they comfort me."* Shepherds do not beat their sheep with the rod and staff to keep them in line. They used it to ward off predators and to guide the sheep, gently bringing them back when they stray. If used to strike the sheep, I doubt David could pen those words so eloquently written in Psalm 23. No one in their right mind could get comfort from the very tool used to inflict physical pain.

I propose that the rod Proverbs speaks of is more connected to creating responsibility and accountability for your child. From that perspective, can we reread these Scripture verses with that idea in mind? If so, each may sound a little like this:

Author remix: "Those who spare the child from *accountability,* hate their children. Those who love their children care enough to discipline them" (Proverbs 13:24, author's paraphrase).

Let's take a look at some New Testament perspectives on parenting: *"Fathers, do not exasperate your children; instead, bring them up in the training and instruction of the Lord"* (Ephesians 6:4 NIV). Or, *"Fathers do not embitter your children, or they will become discouraged"* (Colossians 3:21 NIV). And, *"What do you prefer? Shall I come to you with a rod of discipline, or shall I come in love and with a gentle spirit?"* (1 Corinthians 4:21 NIV).

After reviewing these Scriptures, you can see a display of the Father's heart demonstrating how He desires to love His own children.

Conversation with a Frustrated Mother

I recall a conversation I had with an extremely frustrated mother. She sounded so defeated in the rearing of her four-year-old child. She shared with me, "After five spankings in one day, my child was still repeating the same behaviors he was getting spanked for." She exclaimed, "My God, what is wrong with him!" My first thought was not what's wrong with the child but more in the lines of, *What's wrong with YOU, the parent?* Please forgive me for sounding unempathetic; but Albert Einstein defined insanity as the act of doing the same thing over and over but expecting a different result. Some of our parental actions would most definitely fit into this category. At some point we have to stop, sit back, and really evaluate what we are doing to our kids and why.

My response to that mother was, "Have you invited the Holy Spirit into your disciplining journey with your child? If not, I think it's time."

Rabbit trail warning...

Listen, I knew this particular chapter was going to be controversial and I'm not here to condemn or tell you how to parent your child. My goal is to provide some enlightenment on how some of the behaviors we use against our children have crushed and exacerbated our kids—the very thing the Scriptures warn us not to do.

You may say, "You don't know my children, they are out of control." Again, I am not a child psychologist; but many times children are mirroring the behaviors of the chaotic environments in which they are being raised and developed. Does that apply to your household? Could there potentially be a physical aliment that needs to be addressed? Could there be a different kind of consequence provided to hold your children accountable for their behaviors?

These are just a few ideas that may need to be investigated. But what I can say with 100 percent of surety—we serve an omniscient God who knows all things and desires to co-parent with us. The next time your child rebels, be encouraged to pause and simply ask, "Father, what is the root of this behavior and what are we doing about it?"

As parents, we can't say we love our children if we don't discipline them. Biblical examples of how the Father chastised His children are blueprints for how we are to raise and love our own. One thing I notice about biblical examples is that not all of God's children were disciplined the same way; there is no one template used—and the motive always was love. With this observation, I can't help but conclude that we should not adopt a cookie cutter approach to disciplining our own children either.

I have discovered another revelation—every child and opportunity presenting itself for discipline is an opportunity for heavenly partnership. Now I know what you're thinking, and I agree that this approach does take more time, patience, and most definitely infinite amounts of love. But if the ultimate goal is to raise healthy, emotionally and spiritually balanced children, don't you agree it's worth a try?

What's the Goal?

A mind-set that I believe is healthy to adopt is one that focuses on why you discipline your child. Why does the "why" matter? It matters because many parents do not fully ponder on the desired outcomes. Many parents are only responding out of frustration and anger—which is *never* the right time to discipline your child. So they never really get to the root of the matter.

Let's Go Digging

Parenting with the Holy Spirit ensures you that the root cause of the action can be found. Not every smart-mouthed comment is just your child being thirteen. Not that this behavior is ever acceptable toward an adult, but if you simply respond by isolating the child, taking their phone, spanking them, or jumping back in their face and never discovering the provoking mind-set, emotion or cause, you can be sure that this time will not be the last time you see this response. The goal is always to uproot the reasons behind inappropriate actions.

I currently have a sixteen-year-old and a fourteen-year-old this year, and I have to say that if I can pass the tests being thrown my way, I know that my crown in Heaven is going to be extremely large. Through my own parental journey, I have found that most times when one of my older children is displaying disrespectful behaviors, which I have a zero tolerance for, he or she is dealing with some kind of anger toward me or my husband. When I address the behavior, I follow up with a heartfelt conversation soon afterward. Nine times out of ten, from those conversations exposure of some kind of false perception is revealed or more clarity is provided about what pricked their hearts in an unhealthy way.

As a parent, these steps are repeated over and over throughout your children's teenage years and sometimes beyond. Though tiring at times, you have to keep your eye on the prize—an empty nest—just kidding. The prize is an adult who is walking in purpose, emotionally healthy, spiritually connected to the Father, and confidently loving who they are in Christ.

Don't Be a Bully

Sitting in the mall eating my ice cream minding my own business, I could not help but become distracted by a mother who just kept screaming at her child, who appeared to be about four years old. Every other word was profanity, yelling, and aggressive jumping-in-her-face behaviors. I was so angry and my heart broke for that little person. I saw fear and confusion. The mother kept asking her questions but never gave her a chance to answer because she just jumped in and answered for the little girl.

I wanted to jump up and bully the mother so that she could feel what it felt like, but then I paused and thought, she probably already knows. Any time a person responds to their child that way, they themselves were either treated in like manner or they were never taught how to communicate through the emotions of frustration, anger, and God only knows what else. I said a prayer for both the mother and the child that day, but this story is happening every second of the day in homes around the world.

Human anger does not produce the righteousness God desires (James 1:20 NLT).

As parents, our responsibility is not to beat our children into subjection, control them with anger and fear to do right, or cause an atmosphere in their hearts to be afraid to "mess up." Reacting out of our anger in times of discipline or correction when we feel disrespected can never produce godliness or righteousness in them. What we sow into the hearts of our children will reap that very same harvest. Sowing anger and fear will surely resurface some place in their life as a harvest of anger and fear.

We are all drawn to repentance by the lovingkindness and mercy of God. If God was cruel, mean, unloving, and unkind, what worship could He really expect? If there are behaviors in your child that you find opposite of what you believe they should be displaying, this is an opportunity for you to self-reflect and ask, *What part have I played in these kind of responses? Have I sown a seed into their lives that would reap this kind of harvest?*

I spoke to a renowned child trauma counselor about a young child, age 3, who was displaying very aggressive and troubling behaviors, mirroring oppositional defiant disorder (ODD). Once I explained the backdrop of the child's upbringing to the counselor to see what advice she could provide, her prescription was simple, "You can fix the child by fixing the parents." Children aged 2, 3, 4, and so on, typically mirror behaviors that are being displayed in the home. If children are experiencing trauma, all they have to show in the classroom is trauma. Children living in dysfunction only know how to behave, dysfunctionally. Sadly it's all they know.

A Bully or Leader?

The first demonstration of leadership your child will encounter is from the leadership of their parents or those who are positioned and set in place as guardians over their lives. Their perspective of God and biblical standards will be played out by their parents. If compromise, anger, and control is what kind of leader they experience through you, it will be hard for them to receive a God who is nothing like that. All of their filters of leadership will be through broken or unhealthy lenses that you are presenting to them. Do you know what window they are looking through at this moment?

Parents would be ready to fight any person who bullies their child, never realizing that they themselves could be the very bully their child is hiding from emotionally. Fear-based tactics of raising your children are *not* of God. God would never mandate using a spirit hailing from the kingdom of darkness to keep our kids in line. It's quite the opposite, He would choose perfect love instead.

The following are a few characteristics of Bully Parents vs. Leadership Parents to help you identify and lessen the emotional wounds that many parents cause in the hearts of their young children.

Bully Parent

- Yells and screams at child or in their face.
- Intimidates by point and aggressive face-to-face interactions.
- Uses fear-based tactics.
- Leaves child physically harmed.
- Child is unclear of infraction.
- Anger and or rage is prevalent while correcting the child.
- Demeaning and condescending toward child.
- Child's creative freedom is stifled for fear of making mistakes.
- Parent has no patience with the child.
- Over talks the child, never gives freedom to share.

Leader Parent

- Does not address child's infraction when angry.
- Honors child as a person vs. something to rule over.
- Allows love to be the motive in discipline.

- Ensures children know what they did wrong.
- After discipline, affirms, and builds up the child.
- Has a conversation afterward.
- Child feels safe when sharing true feelings.
- Child explores in a flourishing environment.
- Children feel they are the top priority.
- Child is given time to explain.

Let Love Be the Motive

Growing up, my amazing parents had two different ways of dispensing discipline. My father dispensed discipline from the perspective of spanking and less talking. My mother was more of a communicator and used spanking only as an absolute last resort. From the two of them I have learned so much; but there were many times with my father, whom I love dearly, that I was being disciplined more out of his own frustrations versus getting to the root of the matter.

In contrast to my father, when my mom disciplined me, I would actually feel badly that she was forced to do so. I believe this came from the understanding that my mother would have this deep conversation that started something like this, "Ree," she would call me, "I love you very much, but because you are persistent in being rebellious, I have to spank you." She was as calm as could be, almost in an eerie way. She would kindly share what I did, recall her attempts to stop me from doing it, and further state that she was only spanking me because she loved me. Now mind you, this full conversation was happening while she was spanking my buttocks.

Directly afterward, I would hug her crying out how sorry I was, ultimately looking for affirmation. Not once did she turn me away. She was never disgusted or repelled by me. She would always reaffirm her love and instruct me on how I could have responded differently when asked to change my behavior. Her spankings never felt like abuse or frustration; it felt more like a disciplined action to promote correction.

Right Intention, Horrific Outcome

As I write this chapter, at this very moment, we are going through one of the most trying times of our lives as a family. I have not felt the plague of fear torment my heart for many years until this season crept in so unexpectantly. Though this is challenging for us, I'm asking the Father to provide the reasons behind it all. What lessons are to be learned, and what wisdom can I truly gain and use to grow? Well, first let me explain what we are going through to provide some clarity.

A little over a year ago we received full placement custody of my stepdaughter who at the time of writing this chapter was thirteen years old. This transition into our home was extremely challenging for her and for us. I remember telling her often that she was a hero for having to adjust into a strange place with strange people and strange ways of doing things. For her, it was like being ripped away from all that she knew and held dear. Handling all of this at thirteen years old must have been heart-wrenching for her.

As it connects to disciplining our children, there are countless methods—time out, grounding, extra chores, paddling, cell phones confiscated, no gaming, etc.—that we had used up to the point of this chapter. My husband and I both were paddled as a form of correction growing up and for some children, I believed was an effective means of discipline. Heck, I remember growing up in a Christian private school and received a paddle because I would not go to sleep in kindergarten. To this day, there are private schools that still use paddling as a form of discipline on their students.

WHEN YOUR CHILD FEELS LIKE YOUR ENEMY, THE RESPONSE IS LOVE.

Back to the story.

My stepdaughter was displaying behaviors that completely bent our existing paradigms, and our other children were wincing at her as well. During the time she was living with us, our whole house was completely flipped upside down in ways, to some degree, we are still recovering from. This particular morning started out normal, but ended in a pure nightmare. My older two girls were getting dressed, so I thought. With only ten minutes left before leaving the house, I soon realize that neither of them were ready to go. I was so frustrated because if they were late, that meant I would be late arriving at work, which could not happen yet again.

My husband came home and realized that I had completely given up and decided to "help." He went to the girls' room and all I heard was very disrespectful words being said by one of the girls, followed by some yelling, then two smacks which were proceeded by two young ladies running down the stairs, jumping in the car, and off to school we went. The ride to school was very quiet that morning, both were upset about what took place. After a brief discussion, and I mean *very* brief, I told them I loved them and said, "Try to have a better day."

OK, fast forward. Later that evening I received a call by a representative from the division of social services asking me a whole bunch of questions based on a statement my stepdaughter made claiming that she was physically abused by her father that morning. I recalled to her the same story that you just read, confirmed to the worker that there was no abuse, especially anything resulting in any bruising or anything like that; but despite my affirmation, two days later we found ourselves having to get a lawyer to defend what was said.

More fast forwarding. My husband was officially charged two days later and we were beside ourselves scared. By admitting to smacking his daughter on the buttocks as a means of discipline while using a paddle, according to the state, he broke the very strategically unclear law. You see, in the state of Delaware the laws were changed a few years previous to where it is technically "illegal" to paddle/spank your child. Completely unaware of this change, we fell into the wide net used to catch "real child abusers." But like hundreds of other parents who were nowhere near child abusers, we had to go through the process. Through it all I kept hearing the Father say, "There will be no residue, trust Me."

This story is a long one with a lot of twist and turns, so I will spare you all of the details; but I will say that we never had to go to court, all charges were dropped and dismissed. In the end my stepdaughter told the truth and recanted her story, and our lawyer returned every penny given as a deposit, which never happens. Even though justice was served for us, I literally felt like I got kicked in the emotional stomach. For months I carried around a feeling of nausea, disturbed by what we went through. During those times I remember very distinctly that even though there was so much turmoil, I resisted the urge to "send her back home." I knew in the face of this glaring attack I still needed to love her and learn how to love the person who was trying to destroy us out of her own pain.

In the midst of not knowing the outcome, I told her, "I don't know why you're doing this, but there is nothing you could ever do to make me stop loving you." I was honest with her by telling her that. I then said, "I am heartbroken and confused. It feels like you're trying to destroy the family, but through it all, I will be here for you." Tears filled her eyes, I gave her a hug, and I went into my room and cried. *That day I learned that loving your child at times can be hard, but it's not an excuse to abandon the assignment.*

Parenting Through Tough Times

Not always do we as parents provide instruction and our kids perfectly respond, but that does not let us off the hook from consistently demonstrating love even in tough times. Tough times are not an excuse to abandon those we are entrusted to raise. Yes, we will be frustrated; shoot, so was Jesus, but we must complete the mission in love even when it hurts.

Learn how to cast your cares on the Father, refuel in His love, and go back at it again. Sow grace into your life and the life of your child. Remember, God's mercies are new every day, and this is the standard by which we are to raise our kids. Each day provides new grace and new mercy for them to "get it right." Love keeps no record of wrongs and is patient. Be encouraged to trust God in the journey, and He will keep you to the end.

Another Chat About the Rod

Some people have coined the phrase, "Spare the rod, spoil the child," thinking it is in the Bible. The actual Scripture verse says in the New Living Translation:

> *Those who spare the rod of discipline hate their children. Those who love their children care enough to discipline them.*

Let's study this Scripture a little deeper to get a better understanding of its ever-vast meaning.

I hear many Christians and even myself declaring Proverbs 13:24 because we all generally want our children to do the right thing. So we tout this Scripture and others like it as a justification to not dig deeper and fully understand the metaphoric revelations hidden in the treasure of the Bible's proverbial wisdoms. After doing this study, I have been humbled, changed, and challenged to journey deeper into what Heaven's chastisement really looks like and my prayer is that you begin your own journey as well.

I believe that Proverbs 13:24, along with others like it, could be the most understudied and even misunderstood

Scriptures of all time. Along with Proverbs 13:24, we can also add:

Proverbs 22:15 (NIV) that says, *"Folly is bound up in the heart of a child, but the rod of discipline will drive it far away."* And Proverbs 23:13 (NIV), *"Do not withhold discipline from a child; if you punish them with the rod, they will not die."*

Many people with good intentions implement and take at face value without ever questioning the Scripture's backdrop or if there is a metaphoric understanding or application. When doing a deeper study of Scriptures in the Bible that note the rod, you must look at words proceeding it to get a fuller understanding of its interpretation. For example, the Bible mentions "the rod" and "a rod." I know at first glance you may be wondering, *Who's being that picky...what's the difference?* I'm sure after reading more of this chapter you may change your way of viewing biblical Scriptures over all.

First, I want to say that I did not come to this one revelation solely on my own. I must give credit where credit is due. I was at the door of its discovery when I tripped over an online article written by John K. Rosemond titled "Parenting by the Book," which is really good, by the way. Let's take a look at some of his thoughts on this very matter.

In every case, when the word rod is used with reference to the training or discipline of children, it is preceded by the article the, connoting that the usage is metaphorical. To understand it otherwise results in irreconcilable confusion. For example, in Exodus (21:20), The Lord specifies that if a man beats his male or female slave with a rod, and the slave dies as a direct result, the man must be punished.

Exodus 21:20: *"If a man beats his male or female slave with a rod and the slave dies as a direct result, he must be punished...."*

Speaking in Proverbs (23:13), however, The Lord assures parents that if they punish their children with the rod, "they will not die."

Proverbs 23:13: "Do not withhold discipline from a child; if you punish him with the rod, he will not die."

Reading these two passages, one should be moved to ask, if in fact these two rods are one and the same, how can something that can kill a strong adult slave hold absolutely no potential of being fatal to a child (remember that Proverbs 23:13 is a promise from God Himself!). The only way of reconciling the seeming contradiction is to understand that Exodus refers to an object (a rod), while Proverbs refers to a quality, an attribute (the rod).[1]

What Is Rod-Like Discipline?

Metaphors are used greatly in the Bible and it is our responsibility to partner with the Holy Spirit for the deeper spiritual meanings behind what is really being communicated.

In one context, a rod was used to insure that measurements were consistent and true; in another, it was a symbol of authority, a scepter; and in yet another, as a herding staff, it was used to herd domesticated animals in one general area and compel them to move from one place to another. Used metaphorically, therefore, rod-like discipline (a) is consistent and true, (b) emanates from a legitimate authority, and (c) establishes boundaries and compels action and/or change. Further understanding of the metaphor can be had by noting that "the rod" is also used to refer to God's righteousness, as in Isaiah 11:4, where The Lord is described as smiting the earth with "the rod of his mouth." Rod-like child discipline, therefore, is righteous. It is in keeping with the nature of God's discipline of us, his children both adult and child, and consistent with His Plan for us.[2]

Any discipline delivered out of anger or frustration definitely does not meet the standard of godly discipline. We can take it a step further by saying that particular parent is not responding out of the righteousness of God when any form of discipline is given under the guise of being fed up, angry, control, and fear. Discipline void of love will only breed resentment and contempt in the heart of your child, thus eventually backfiring because it will feel more like abuse.

The idea of beating your child into subjection is flawed to the core. This is a fear-based model that most times only causes your child to learn how to manipulate because fear controls and control manipulates. They will learn to behave in your presence out of fear; but if the grand idea is to train, educate, build up, and empower your child to live a prosperous life, why not seek a godly perspective on discipline that is supported by the One who never fails.

Ephesians 6:4 says, *"Fathers, do not exasperate your children; instead, bring them up in the training and instruction of the Lord."*

I would like to present an idea that "the rod" that the Scriptures instructs us to use is also known as a healthy leadership model that grows and matures your children without breaking them deep inside. Healthy leadership in the home will foster healthier kids. From this study I have found that many parents do not necessarily need "parenting classes" but rather the potential for leadership development.

Points to Ponder

- The Holy Spirit desires to parent with you.
- Discipline is necessary for a child to develop and mature.
- Never discipline your child while angry.
- Seek the root cause of your child's behavior.
- Make sure the children understand why they are being disciplined.
- Teach your child the value of receiving feedback.
- Make sure *love* is the motive of your discipline.
- Let the leader in you arise while you disciple your child.
- Remember your assignment is to lead and train your child in the way they should go.

Discipline Tips

- Have your children come up with some consequences for when they break the rules.
- Make sure your children clearly understand what's expected of them.
- Ensure that the consequence fits the infraction.
- Remove anger from the equation.
- Pray for grace and patience while parenting.
- Ask the Holy Spirit, "What are we doing here?"

Let's Play "Do I?"

Provide your child with this questionnaire and ask them to be as honest as possible when answering. Based on the score, you may have some work to do in the way you communicate to your child and others. Remember, there is no condemnation if your score reflects you need to go to the "ER." Feedback is an opportunity for you and your child to grow and mature.

DO I?		
0 point for every "NO" & 1 point for every "YES" *(Please answer based on how the person responds "most of the time")*	NO	YES
Do I tend to yell during communicating?		
Do I bait my listener in an attempt to "get them" (Set people up during conversations)?		
Do I aggressively tell people what to do?		
Do I tend to control conversation; do I not accept other people's decisions?		
Do I point or use threatening gestures?		
Do I cut people off while talking?		
Do I tend to mention what I've done to validate my point(s)?		
Do I accuse others without having all the fact?		
Do I patiently listen to fully understand another's view? *(If yes—0 point, if no—1 point)*		
Do I generally speak through hurt, pain, regret, negative filters, etc.?		
TOTAL:		
Final Score:		
SCORE KEY· Total up all		
0	Wow! You're close to Jesus! :)	
1	Skillfully mindful of others	
2	Very mindful of others	
3	Generally mindful of others	
4	Need some work	
5	Go to the family doctor	
6 and up	Urgent care is needed, go to the "ER" and on your way buy some duct tape	

ENDNOTES

1. John K. Rosemond, "Parenting by The Book," http://www .parentingbythebook.com/Proverbs-1324.html; accessed December 24, 2019.

2. Ibid.

Chapter Ten

LOVE, THE MOST POWERFUL TOOL ON EARTH

Love is a weapon. Love is the most powerful tool and weapon against the enemy on earth. It is the one concept the enemy cannot comprehend, understand, or ever receive. Love is and will always be the vehicle used by heaven to constantly undermine and debilitate the schemes of our adversary. Love should always be the fuel used when attempting to bring our children into alignment. Loving your child the way they receive and need to be loved is one of the greatest weapons against the works of the enemy in their lives. Knowing you are wanted and loved provides a level of security that if valued the child will live from healthy filters versus ones that cause you to compromise only to gain validation.

Even Science Supports the Need for Love

The power of love is backed up by science. Scientific studies are always a helpful reaffirmation of how important it is to practice lovingkindness and shower the people you love with love.

A new study from UCLA suggests that a loving parental figure may alter neural circuits in children that
could influence health throughout a lifespan. On the
flip side, the negative impact of childhood abuse or
lack of parental affection take a mental and physical
toll that can also last a lifetime. Childhood neglect
increases adult risk for morbidity and mortality.

The September 2013 study, titled "Childhood Abuse,
Parental Warmth, and Adult Multisystem Biological
Risk in the Coronary Artery Risk Development
in Young Adults Study" is published online by the
Proceedings of the National Academy of Sciences.
This study is the first time researchers have exam-
ined the effects of abuse and lack of parental affection
across the human body's entire regulatory system, and
found a strong biological link between negative early
life experiences and poor health later in life.

"Our findings suggest that there may be a way to
reduce the impact abuse has, at least in terms of physical health," said Judith E. Carroll, a research scientist
at the Cousins Center for Psychoneuroimmunology
at UCLA, and the study's lead author. "If the child
has love from parental figures they may be more protected from the impact of abuse on adult biological
risk for health problems than those who don't have
that loving adult in their life."

Many previous reports on childhood abuse or neglect
have found a link between a child's psychological and
physical well-being. For instance, "toxic" childhood

stress has been linked to elevated cholesterol, cardiovascular disease, metabolic syndrome and other physical conditions posing a significant health risk. The researchers suggest that toxic childhood stress alters neural responses to stress, boosting the emotional and physical arousal to threat and making it more difficult for that reaction to be shut off.[1]

After reading this article, I ran and gave my kids tens hugs each and said a prayer for all the little ones in the world who don't feel loved.

Now that you are aware that to remain physically healthy your child needs love, the next question is how does your child receive love? Do you know how your child receives love?

Story Time

Sarah cried profusely as she spouted to her mother how she never felt loved growing up as a child and now she struggles with loving her own children. She went on to say that she felt like the outcast in the family and no one really spent any time with her. Being one of six children, she resolved in her heart that what she had to say growing up was never as important as what her younger brother had to say who always seemed to get everyone's attention.

Now an adult, Sarah could no longer hold the pain inside, so she laid it all out on the line twenty-five years later to her mother, ultimately saying that she "never felt loved by her or anyone." Sarah's mother was shocked beyond belief, she worked her fingers to the bone ensuring Sarah went to ballet lessons, paid for her to go on all the school field trips, and she even purchased Sarah's wedding dress. Sarah's mother wondered, *How could Sarah ever believe those horrible lies of the enemy?*

This scenario is not unusual nor uncommon, especially in large-size families. The fact of the matter is that people tend to give love according to how they receive it. If you desire people in your life to buy you things to prove their love, more than likely you too will be a giver of things. The question is, what happens when things just don't do it for the other person?

Could Sarah be a victim of misappropriation of love? Based on Sarah's summary, it appears that she may be a "quality time" person; and because her mother constantly worked to buy her things, Sarah's love bucket remained constantly empty.

The idea that people have specific "love languages" is a fairly new concept introduced in our generation. I emphatically would like to thank Gary Chapman for this revelation defined in his book titled, *Five Love Languages*. Though I was introduced to this theory from a marital perspective, I instinctively applied the same lessons learned to my kids, which created major changes in the way I parented and loved them.

You do not know what you do not know, and you cannot fix what you do not have a clue is broken. When you know better, you do better; so please do not condemn yourself if a lot of what I'm saying is new. Today is always a good day to start over. I am still on a daily journey to love my kids the way they desire and need to receive love so that their love buckets can be overflowing with, well, love.

How Do You Need Me to Love You?

When children know, understand, and feel they are loved, another level of security is encamped around their hearts making the fiery darts of the enemy less effective—and in many cases impenetrable. How do they want to be rewarded and praised? What hurts them about the way they are currently parented? What can you do as their parent to make them 100 percent say they are loved by you?

What's the Point?

The point is, the way God loves us is how we should love our children. God's ways of fathering provides us a model—that no matter how many times we or our children make mistakes, fall, and fail, He never condemns and His love is always unconditional toward us. Likewise, your children should always know they have a safe place with you. That the home of your heart will always have room in it for them to dwell. Knowing they have a safe place to emotionally land adds value and builds identity in the hearts of your children. No matter how hard the journey gets with your child, love will always conquer any hell in them—as it did in you.

Loving Your Pre-Born Child

I want to turn your attention to an idea that may be a little strange to you—loving your child from the womb. This book is not just recommended for parents, but for parents-to-be as well.

Don't wait until your children are born to shower love upon them by speaking life, affirmations, and blessings. From inception to the birthing moment, your child has a spirit that can be affected by what's being poured into it, way before the child's intellect catches up.

And it happened, when Elizabeth heard the greeting of Mary, that the babe leaped in her womb; and

Elizabeth was filled with the Holy Spirit (Luke 1:41 NKJV).

I believe that from the womb children can divinely sense God. When Elizabeth (the mother of John the Baptist) and Mary (the mother of Jesus) came into close proximity of each other while they were both pregnant, the Bible says the baby leapt in Elizabeth's womb. This is an exciting revelation because what I understand from this story is that even from the womb we can perceive the presence of God. If we are able to perceive and have emotion from the womb, isn't that part of what makes us alive? In order to discern God, there has to be a mind and spirit; and in this particular case, the emotion of what was discerned literally caused a physical reaction, in the womb! Mind, body, and soul were proven to be fully displayed in that one verse.

Now knowing this I scratch my head every time a debate breaks out on whether or not an unborn baby is just a lump of organs versus a real human being. I believe willful blindness plays a major part in any narrative that supports the lump of organ stance because there is too much evidence proving that even in the womb babies have been known to cry, show emotion, smile, and demonstrate the same kind of behaviors they do outside of the womb.

If we can perceive God, then the next assumption would be is that we can also perceive evil or darkness. So the protective covering process for our children should not start on their delivery day—create distance from the enemy and get a head start by even interceding while you are just thinking about having kids. Pray over and begin to love the children you do not yet have!

I was about seven months pregnant with my third child, Mycah Elyse, when I was awakened out of a deep sleep by God's voice saying with urgency, "War for the life of your baby." Now I know that may sound a bit dramatic, but it happened just like that. I had so many questions after I heard God, but I was obedient to the Voice even though not fully understanding what was taking place. I may never know the answer about what was going on in the spirit realm, but what I do know is that she's now nine years old and I attribute that to hearing a still small voice and obeying.

Conceiving Mycah was a bit of a challenge. While carrying her, at one point my placenta was competing for room to grow with an extremely large fibroid. The doctors were majorly concerned that it would outgrow my sack and eventually abort my baby. Hearing those words felt like someone shot an arrow straight through heart. My response was not stuck on disaster, quite the opposite; every day until I saw a change I cursed that fibroid and spoke life to my baby. I prayed, "She is stronger than what is trying to over-power her. No weapon formed against her will prosper," and so much more.

F.Y.I. Prayer works; I have a nine-year-old today as living to proof.

Though this particular pregnancy was very challenging, I continued to speak life daily. My overall prayer for my children is that while in the womb, like John the Baptist, they would experience and be encountered by the presence of God. While in the womb, I constantly covered them with worship music and sang over them because while they developed into who they were going to be, I wanted the Spirit of God to get down deep into the DNA of who they were.

It's Never Too Late

You may say, I missed this level of opportunity to cover my baby in the womb in this manner. Do not fear—it's never too late. Whether your child is one or seventeen years old, today is always the right day to introduce them to heavenly atmospheres and biblical teachings that will foundationally support them into becoming all they can become.

> *I knew you before I formed you in your mother's womb.*
> *Before you were born I set you apart and appointed you*
> *as my prophet to the nations* (Jeremiah 1:5 NLT).

God told Jeremiah that before he was in his mother's womb He knew him. This sets a precedent that every one of your children has a gift and calling on their lives, and from the womb Heaven is watching, waiting, and expecting that call to be realized in the earth realm.

Like God, the enemy also wants to encounter your child from the womb. From the Bible days until now, satan plans to murder our children before they can become a threat to his kingdom. Unfortunately, this concept of massive child killings and baby sacrificing is not new. The goal of the enemy is to murder the King while he is still a kid. The methods are the only thing that have changed. More than 2,000 years ago he sent out armies to murder all first-born sons, and today he is using murder by a monstrous demonic procedure known as abortion that kills sons and daughters.

You would think that living in some far off war-torn country would be the most dangerous place for a child to live today—but according to studies, the most dangerous place for a child to live now is in the mother's womb. Studies show that more babies of a particular race were aborted in New York City than were allowed to be born. I hope that tragic reality provokes you to pray for all babies in the womb.

ALWAYS SEEK TO UNDERSTAND THROUGH THE SPIRIT OF LOVE VERSUS LAW AND CONDEMNATION.

Love Is Forgiveness

As a parent raising children, at times this can seem to be one of the hardest responsibilities to work through. Just because you're a parent does not mean you will not get hurt by your kids or even have feelings of disappointment. We have expectations of our children; and when they intentionally or unintentionally do not meet them, let's just say it's not the best feeling in the world. We have to learn how to exercise forgiveness, even toward our children.

Forgiveness Is a weapon

Demonstrating forgiveness toward our children is one of the greatest lessons we could ever teach them. Choosing to forgive others is not just a choice, it's a humble demonstration of the realization that we too have been forgiven. It's one of the greatest pay-it-forward acts of humanity ever to be displayed.

Scriptures teach us that when we were in our most filthy, hellish state, Jesus died to redeem us. Being perfect was not the prerequisite of being saved. *"While we were still sinners, Christ died for us"* (Romans 5:8 NIV). My righteousness is as a filthy rag to God, and even my good deeds are being fueled by God's desires in me. I can't even take credit for that. My point in telling all of this is simple, we have no cause to self-righteously hold our children to standards only Jesus can keep, and not forgive them when they come up short. The goal is to model forgiveness time and time again until for your child it becomes a learned behavior response.

LEARN TO LET GO—FORGIVENESS IS A WEAPON.

Simply put, forgiveness is the act of pardoning an offender. It is not contingent on feeling like it or even if you think the person deserves your forgiveness. It does not mean that the person being forgiven does not deserve punishment—it's a spiritual ability to see at one point that you were forgiven so you choose to forgive.

In the Bible, the Greek word translated "forgiveness" literally means "to let go," to decide to let go of what was done to you so that you can be free from the offense.

Over and over forgiveness can be taught to your child. First by extending it to them and telling them you are forgiving them; and second by walking them through it when they themselves are having a hard time letting go of an offense.

Unforgiveness Opens Doors to Evil

Teaching your child how to forgive quickly heads off attacks and opening access points to the enemy. It also frees them up to be able to live in prosperity and partake in the benefits of God's Kingdom, which are righteousness, peace, and joy.

Unforgiveness is one of the main doors that provides access for the enemy to be able to legally infiltrate our lives and the lives of our children. God's Word teaches us that when we choose not to forgive others, we can then be given over to a tormenting spirit (Matthew 18:32-34). Since evil spirits like to travel in packs, we have to understand that choosing not to forgive invites the spirits of bitterness, discontentment, rage, unrest, confusion, rebellion and torment.

Most times when we are wrestling with forgiving someone, we find ourselves being tormented by the incident, playing it over and over in our minds. Then we begin to have mental conversations with our offender about what we really want to say or even "giving them a piece of our minds." The offense goes deep down causing soulish torments brought on by what we won't let go of. Forgiveness is so important because once we forgive, it breaks the chain that mentally keeps us latched to the person who wounded us.

It's crucial to teach our children that forgiveness is our response to a loving merciful God and has nothing to do with if someone deserves to be forgiven. The following revelation must be a real revelation to their hearts: all people have sinned and come short of ever "earning" God's glorious love. With this understanding, how can we feel justified in holding someone else in chains for what they have done?

Story Time

Being a pastor who does some emotional trauma counseling, I get to journey with so many people and hear stories that at times just breaks my heart. This particular story involves a counseling session with a teenager who had gone through a lot of pain involving abuse, neglect, and a lot of rejection. Meeting with him week after week working through the pains of his life, it became very apparent to me and the other counselor that forgiveness was the wall preventing him from experiencing any peace.

Each session we broke down forgiveness—what it was and who it was for—but he still adamantly refused. He did not want to understand that though he was wronged, vengeance was God's to repay. He felt that if he held on to the anger and the offense, it would ensure the other person's punishment. He was completely blind of seeing that what he was holding on to was tearing him apart inside. Unforgiveness became a toxic disease he suffered with daily. The saddest part about this story? Wholeness could have been restored in his life if only he would let go.

If you were holding a rope and someone set it on fire at one end, the most natural thing for you to do is let go of the rope so that you aren't burned right? As simple as that seems, many are bound up and burned on the inside as a result of not wanting to let go.

Teaching your child how to let go can save them from years of being bound up inside as an adult. Being angry and even upset about not being treated fairly is not the sin, but it becomes sin once we harden our hearts to forgive the one who trespassed against us.

For if you forgive other people when they sin against you, your heavenly Father will also forgive you. But if you do not forgive others their sins, your Father will not forgive your sins. (Matthew 6:14-15)

A good lesson connected to forgiveness is trusting God. Teach your children that their heavenly Father will dispense justice. He defends the weak and is very clear that payback is His alone. When *we* decide how a person should be punished, we attempt to take the place of the only One who is holy, pure, and true enough to dispense perfect justice. Teach your children that they can trust God because the only thing God *cannot* do, is fail them.

Points to Ponder

- Love is the most powerful tool on earth.
- Learning how your child receives love is crucial.
- Love creates space to make mistakes.

- Loving your child in the womb is possible.
- Love is forgiveness.
- Forgiveness is a weapon.
- Forgiveness shuts the door to the tormentor.

Chapter Activation

Take time to chat with your children and uncover what's really going on deep down inside. Walk them through forgiving anyone they could possibly be holding any grudges against, even if it's you.

Secondly, if you do not know, it's time to find out how your child receives love. To assist with this, have your child take the Five Love Language test for kids. Using the results from the Five Love Language test for kids (online test link under the tool kit section in this book), you will now have practical ways to begin journeying with your child in building a stronger foundation on an intentional love connection.

In addition to your child taking the test, it is also good to simply ask your children what makes them feel loved and special—that way you are hearing directly from them.

ENDNOTE

1. Christopher Bergland, "Parental Warmth Is Crucial for a Child's Well-Being," *Psychology Today, October 4, 2013;* https://www .psychologytoday.com/us/blog/the-athletes-way/201310/parental -warmth-is-crucial-child-s-well-being; accessed December 26, 2019.

CONVERSATION STARTER TIPS

Stop Simply Asking, "How Was Your Day?"

We can miss so much by asking our children cookie cutter questions in an attempt to find out how their day went. Kids typically will say, "Good," when asked "How was your day?" But as the parent, you want to know how they are *really* doing. The following are some suggested conversation starters that hopefully will allow you to get to know your child even better.

- "Anything interesting happened today?"
- "You appear a little frustrated, anything agitate you today?"
- "During class, are you able to stay focused?"
- "Anything really cool happen today?"
- "How is _____ (insert child's friend(s) name) doing?"
- "Any teachers you really like or dislike? Why?"
- "On a scale of one to five, how smart do you think you are?"

- "How comfortable are you with sharing with me when you are really upset?"
- "Who do you feel comfortable talking to?"
- "Do you feel like your opinions matter or are heard?"
- "What was the funniest part of your day today?"
- "Anybody make you angry today?"
- "You seem a little sad, anything I can do to cheer you up?"
- "How much sleep do you get at night?" Or, "Do you wake up during the middle of the night?"
- "What do you like or dislike about your school?"
- "Do you feel you are being treated fairly at home and at school?"

By asking my children some of the above questions, I found out: one was being bullied, another was just asked out by a guy, and having major issues with a teacher. The list goes on and on.

Get creative and add some of your own. As the parent it's very important that you ask open-ended questions to allow for dialog. Become an investigator of their emotions and thinking. During these conversations you are adding seeds of value into their lives by letting them know they matter and that you care enough to ask them about their day in strategic ways. Always listen to their answers and take time to hear what they are really saying.

Have fun!

RESOURCE TOOL BOX

The following are suggested resources, some of which were mentioned in the book. Having a slew of credible go-to resources to assist you on your parenting journey is important. Two resources I love to highlight are:

First, "Story time with Grandmom." This is an online subscription-based tool that allows your child to get Sunday school type lessons from a character named, "Grandmom." Your child will learn not only Bible stories but also how to deal practically with challenges they are facing today.

Second is, Nikao. Nikao is a spiritual warfare family board game that I created, set to be released October 2020. The Nikao board game will empower your child with Scriptures, tools, and strategies on how to extinguish the fiery darts of the enemy they may face in their everyday lives.

Resources and Links

*Story time with Grand-mom: www.storytimewithgrandmom
.com

*NIKAO board game www.nikaogame.com (Coming September
2020)

Love language test for kids by Gary Chapman: https://www
.5lovelanguages.com/profile/?child#discovery-child; accessed
December 26, 2019.

Battlefield of the Mind: Winning the Battle in Your Mind by Joyce
Meyer (New York: Warner Faith 2002).

Online Complete Topical Scripture Guide: https://www
.biblestudytools.com/topical-verses/.

Rules of Engagement by Cindy Trimm (Lake Mary, FL: Charisma
House 2008).

A FEW WORDS EXPLAINED

Halloween (definition from History.com)

"Halloween's origins date back to the ancient Celtic festival of Samhain (pronounced sow-in). The Celts, who lived 2,000 years ago, mostly in the area that is now Ireland, the United Kingdom and northern France, celebrated their new year on November 1. This day marked the end of summer and the harvest and the beginning of the dark, cold winter, a time of year that was often associated with human death. Celts believed that on the night before the New Year, the boundary between the worlds of the living and the dead became blurred. On the night of October 31 they celebrated Samhain, when it was believed that the ghosts of the dead returned to earth. In addition to causing trouble and damaging crops, Celts thought that the presence of the other-worldly spirits made it easier for the Druids, or Celtic priests, to make predictions about the future. For a people entirely depen-dent on the volatile natural world, these prophecies were an important source of comfort during the long, dark winter. To commemorate the event, Druids built huge sacred bonfires, where the people gathered to burn crops and animals as sacrifices to the

Celtic deities. During the celebration, the Celts wore costumes, typically consisting of animal heads and skins, and attempted to tell each other's fortunes. When the celebration was over, they re-lit their hearth fires, which they had extinguished earlier that evening, from the sacred bonfire to help protect them during the coming winter."

Magic (definition from Merriam-Webster)

"The use of means (such as charms or spells) believed to have supernatural power over natural forces; magic rites or incantations; an extraordinary power or influence seemingly from a supernatural source." The ability through supernatural powers to cast spells and perform influence over a person, place, or thing.

Witchcraft (definition from Merriam-Webster)

"One who the use of sorcery or magic; communication with the devil or with a familiar." The craft of communicating with the devil or a familiar spirit.

Medium (definition from Merriam-Webster)

"An individual held to be a channel of communication between the earthly world and a world of spirits." This individual claims to be able to speak to the spirits of the dead. This is necromancy (an abomination in the sight of God to speak to the dead). They are also known as channelers.

Divination (definition from Merriam-Webster)

"The art or practice that seeks to foresee or foretell future events or discover hidden knowledge usually by the interpretation of omens or by the aid of supernatural powers." Divination is similar to witchcraft being that it is fuel by the kingdom of darkness.

godly prophets prophesy out of the Spirit of God, fortune tellers attempt to tell the future from spirits of darkness.

All Seeing Eye aka Eye of Horus

Horus was the ancient Egyptian sky god who was usually depicted as a falcon, most likely a lanner or peregrine falcon. His right eye was associated with the sun god, Ra. The eye symbol represents the marking around the eye of the falcon, including the "teardrop" marking sometimes found below the eye. The mirror image, or left eye, sometimes represented the moon and the god Djehuti (Thoth).

The Eye of Horus, also known as wadjet, wedjat or udjat

An ancient Egyptian symbol of protection, royal power, and good health. The Eye of Horus is similar to the Eye of Ra, which belongs to a different god, Ra, but represents many of the same concepts.

It was believed by the Greeks and Romans that an evil heart could get to the eye. The thought to be powerful effects of eyes and optics created the myth that the energy-producing power of the eye had the ability to cast evil spells with just a glance. Because the ancients believed the evil eye could be counteracted with a good eye, myths about Horus arose.

TOPICAL SCRIPTURE GUIDE

There is a helpful online tool that provides a complete Scripture topical guide for you to use as a reference (link provided on Resource Tool Box page). The following is a compilation of Scriptures based on major themes discussed in the book. Enjoy discovering the Bible, God's Word, in a personal, meaningful way.

FEAR
Isaiah 35:4
John 14:27
John 1:9
Matthew 6:34
1 John 4:18
Isaiah 43:1

ANXIETY/WORRY
Isaiah 40:31
John 14:1
Luke 12:22
Matthew 6:24-34
Psalm 94:19

FORGIVENESS
Colossians 3:13
Luke 17:3-4
Ephesians 4:31-32
Numbers 14:19-21
Mark 11:25

ANGER
Ephesians 4:26-31
James 1:19-20
Proverbs 29:11
Proverbs 19:11
Proverbs 15:1
Colossians 3:8

BULLYING
Deuteronomy 31:6
Matthew 5:11
Leviticus 19:18
Psalm 138:7

LOVE
John 3:16
Romans 5:8
1 John 4:8
John 15:13

DISCIPLINE	SUFFERING/TRAILS	PEACE
Ephesians 6:4	1 Peter 3:14	Colossians 3:15
Proverbs 10:17	2 Timothy 3:12	Galatians 5:22
Proverbs 12:1	Colossians 1:24	Hebrews 12:14
Proverbs 13:1	Isaiah 43:2	1 Peter 5:7
Proverbs 22:6	James 1:12	James 3:18
FAITH	**JOY**	Romans 14:19
1 John 5:5	2 John 1:12	**IDENTITY**
1 John 5:13	Psalm 27:6	John 1:12
Galatians 2:20	Psalm 47:1	Genesis 1:27
James 1:6	Isaiah 9:3	1 Peter 2:9
Matthew 17:20	Romans 15:13	1 Corinthians 6:19-20
	Philemon 1:7	1 John 3:1-2
		Ephesians 1:5

SOURCES CITED

Jones, Kidada. *School of Awake* (San Francisco, CA: New World Library, 2017).

Silk, Danny. *Unpunishable: Ending Our Love Affair with Punishment* (El Dorado Hills, CA: Loving On Purpose, 2019).

Rosemond, John K. "Parenting by the book," *Psychology Today,* October 4, 2013; https://www.psychologytoday.com/us /blog/ the-athletes-way/ 201310/parental-warmth-is-crucial-child-s-well -being; accessed October 2, 2019.

Slick, Matt. "What is a familiar spirit"; Christian Apologetics & Research Ministry; https://carm.org/what-is-a-familiar-spirit; accessed December 26, 2019.

Stone Jr., Perry. *Feeding Demons* (Austin, TX: The Fedd Agency, Inc., 2017).

Definitions:

Charlie Charlie Challenge: https://en.wikipedia.org/wiki/Charlie _Charlie _challenge; accessed October 2019.

Divination: https://www.merriam-webster.com/dictionary/divination; accessed December 26, 2019.

Halloween: https://www.history.com/topics/halloween/history-of -halloween; accessed December 26, 2019.

Magic: https://www.merriam-webster.com/dictionary/magic.

Medium: https://www.merriam-webster.com/dictionary/medium.

Witchcraft: https://www.merriam-webster.com/dictionary/witchcraft.

Eye of Horus: https://en.wikipedia.org/wiki/Eye_of_Horus accessed
January 5, 2020.

ABOUT THE AUTHOR

Sharee Dorsett is an author, worship leader, recording artist, and co-pastor of City of Love Church in Wilmington, Delaware.

Sharee is known by her peers as an equipper of leaders and an innovator, which was highlighted when she was awarded with the Business Times' "Delaware's top 40 under 40 leaders." She loves to push others in their purpose and help expand people's ability to creatively launch and expand their businesses and ministries.

She is married to Arnold Dorsett and they have four children. Sharee's oldest son, Kamryn, at two years of age came under spiritual attack, which began her journey of equipping children in spiritual warfare—the major catalyst to writing *Small but Mighty*.

Sharee prides herself in serving her family and equipping her children to live out of their God-given authority and purpose. One of her greatest passions in life is helping others find their purpose and being a vessel used to help others see themselves through God's eyes.

Contact Information

Ministry Websites: https://shareedorsettonline.com
https://cityoflovechurch.com
shareedorsett.info@gmail.com
https://www.facebook.com/@ShareeDorsett